THE PEACH
AND THE COCONUT

A GUIDE TO COLLABORATION
FOR GLOBAL TEAMS

Scott C. Hammond, Ph.D.,
Danny Damron, Ph.D., and
Christopher Liechty

ARCHWAY
PUBLISHING

Archway Publishing books may be ordered through booksellers or by contacting:

Archway Publishing
1663 Liberty Drive
Bloomington, IN 47403
www.archwaypublishing.com
1 (888) 242-5904

Because of the dynamic nature of the Internet, any web addresses or links contained in this book may have changed since publication and may no longer be valid. The views expressed in this work are solely those of the author and do not necessarily reflect the views of the publisher, and the publisher hereby disclaims any responsibility for them.

ISBN: 978-1-4808-6619-5 (sc)
ISBN: 978-1-4808-6618-8 (e)

Library of Congress Control Number: 2018909227

Print information available on the last page.

Archway Publishing rev. date: 10/17/2018

CONTENTS

INTRODUCTION

A wise storyteller recounts the tale of an inmate in a Chinese prison who took tiny wires from the floor of the labor shop and put them in a glass bottle over many long years of confinement. One day he was freed. He took with him only the bottle to help him remember the long years of forced labor.

The former prisoner was now too old to work, but each day he arose at the exact time the prison had required. And each day he spent his hours walking in his room exactly as he had in his prison cell, taking four steps forward and four steps back, four steps forward and four steps back, four steps forward and four steps back. Author Bette Bao Lord, who penned this story, tells what happened when the prisoner finally broke the bottle to see how many wires he had accumulated: "He wept. At his feet lay broken glass, and a clump of wires rusted solid in the shape of a bottle."[1]

We all have rusted wires, well-worn paths that shape our behavior. They are our most deeply held habits, unquestioned and sometimes unseen. We rarely walk these paths alone. We learn to follow them by watching those closest to us: our families, friends, and communities. We call these paths culture.

Every community has a culture—even a prison, a corporation, or a university. Culture imprints our behaviors and gives us rational shortcuts so we can move forward without asking difficult "why" questions about everything we do. Our wires are rusted into different shapes, but those shapes are all that we know, so our own cultures are most often invisible to us. But they are always there, shaping our actions and behaviors.

The further we get from our most immediate and familiar communities, the more we see differences. When we cross a cultural border, we sometimes see something that is so different that we feel disoriented, confused, or even angry. Why would someone be that way? Why do they think like that or speak like that? This disorientation becomes acute when business, education, or even pleasure places us squarely in front of cultural differences, forcing us into situations where we must be productive with those who are least like us.

In the classic response, we tend to respond to these perceived threats by choosing either fight or flight. We may mock others, call them dangerous, or insist that they be more like us. We may try to make them play by our rules or assimilate. Or we may simply run away and not deal with the differences. Over human history, the fight-or-flight response has kept us safe from wild animals but has not produced much that is sustainable.

A third option is to find another way—not "your way" or "my way," but a way we create together. Based on academic research and decades of experience working in global teams, we have developed a method called Culture3 Dialogue. It is a plan for building a bridge, a way for members of multicultural teams to transcend their own cultures without giving them up. It is anchored in "your culture" and "my culture," but together the teammates establish a third culture, "our culture." In time, it can become a bridge among teammates that they own, share, and walk together.

This book will help you understand your own cultural preferences. It will help you see how others are different and why. And it will help you build a way of seeing and communicating that can lead to productive business; deeper learning; and enduring, fruitful relationships with people who were once outsiders, rivals, or even enemies.

To accomplish these goals, you must do more than read this book. By applying these ideas to the workings of a global team, to international travel, or to an educational experience, you will be doing the hard and rewarding work of cultural bridge building. This labor has a long-term reward. You will see yourself differently as you come to realize how others see you. You will see others differently as you come to understand their deepest values. And you will begin to bridge the cultural gap between yourself and others, reaping the rich rewards of a global age.

CHAPTER 1
First Encounters: The Challenge of Culture

Yongju Lee had been in the United States less than twenty-four hours on his new job assignment, and he already wanted to return home to South Korea. It wasn't the lack of familiar food or the new work environment or the absence of a set schedule. He was amazed that in such a short time, multiple people had treated him with a complete lack of respect for his experience, ideas, and background. Everyone was so informal, and he couldn't figure out how to fit in.

Yongju was part of an expensive, high-priority, company-wide exchange program. This strategy had been developed to create better relationships among employees from different countries and to reduce significant miscommunication and errors that were occurring among company divisions in various regions of the world. Though Yongju had been preparing for this assignment for months, he could hardly believe what had happened just in one day abroad.

Yongju had arrived on a Sunday evening in a medium-sized Midwestern town after twenty-two hours of traveling. After the chaos of immigration and customs checks, he was ready to relax on the drive from the airport. As he walked into the airport's receiving area, he scanned the name placards that people were holding up. Not seeing his name, he looked more carefully but still didn't see it. After waiting forty-five minutes for his driver, he tried calling his company's local administrative assistant. She did not answer, even though he had received an email from her that said, "If you have any questions, please feel free to call."

Not knowing what else to do, Yongju joined several other people milling around in front of the kiosk labeled "Information" to get some help. When Yongju finally got to the counter, the attendant was on the phone and just pointed her index finger in his direction without saying anything. She eventually finished her call, but before Yongju could ask for help, another man jumped in front of him to ask where the nearest restroom was. When Yongju finally got the attendant's attention, he asked for directions to his hotel. She said she hadn't heard of that hotel.

Now really flustered, Yongju wandered outside the airport terminal.

At this point, he happened to see an airport shuttle with his hotel's name on the side. Hoping this would be the end of his troubles, he dragged his heavy bag up the shuttle steps. To Yongju's surprise, the driver didn't offer to help or even welcome him. Instead, he just remained sitting. Yongju hefted his bag into the luggage rack himself and sat down.

As he relaxed on the ride into the city, Yongju looked forward to meeting his colleagues, who would surely be waiting for him at the hotel. But no one was waiting in the lobby when he checked in. He did, however, receive a message from the administrative assistant that said he would be having "dinner on his own" that night.

In the morning, Yongju ate a continental breakfast alone in the hotel lobby. Guessing that there wouldn't be a car to take him to the office, he hailed a cab and found his way there. He felt encouraged when a sharply dressed young man greeted him in the lobby and rode the elevator with him up to his floor. Unfortunately, Yongju's cubical was not ready, so he was placed in an empty conference room. The young man told him that orientation would begin soon and to "just wait," then left. After Yongju had waited an hour, a group walked in for a scheduled meeting. He found his way across the hall to another empty conference room. His visit had been planned for months, yet his arrival seemed to be a complete surprise.

In his first team meeting that afternoon, Yongju was introduced to the entire marketing team. They, in turn, quickly introduced themselves and jumped right into the day's business. That was when Yongju became angry. He was a senior marketing professional on a six-month assignment from the Asian division, and these people were talking about the Asian market as though he was not even in the room. He sat in silence, politely waiting to be invited into the conversation. The invitation never came.

As the meeting broke up, several members of the team greeted Yongju. They talked loudly and slowly, as if he could not understand English, then promised to have lunch with him during his stay. No one asked for his opinion or offered to involve him in any part of the project, so he returned to his temporary "office" with nothing to do. This was going to be a long six months, he thought.

Meanwhile, Cassandra Hayes and Jim Thorton were arriving in South Korea from the company's US headquarters to spend six months in the Asian division. Cassandra (a product-development director) and Jim (one of her team members) had been preparing for the stint abroad by learning about Korean food and geography. They had even gotten some language instruction and were prepared to accept business cards and gifts with both hands. But when they got off the plane, the new culture hit them in the face.

Thinking they would have the remainder of the day to prepare to make a good first impression, they planned to take a taxi to their hotel and rest. But to their surprise, they were greeted at the airport by a young woman who identified herself as the "host" and administrative assistant for the department where they would be working.

"Ms. Hayes, Mr. Thorton," said the host. "Welcome to Korea."

"Please, feel free to call me Cassandra," Cassandra said.

"And I'm Jim," Jim added.

"Yes, Ms. Hayes, Mr. Thorton," said the host.

She escorted Cassandra and Jim to a luxury car, where the trio and a company driver set off for the hotel. Somewhere in the polite conversation along the way, it became clear that it was the "host's duty" to deliver Jim to a restaurant in the downtown area, where there was to be a gathering of peers and colleagues. They stopped at the hotel and dropped off Jim's luggage. Cassandra was escorted to her room by the host, and Jim was whisked away by the driver, who did not speak English.

Bleary-eyed and unshaven after the long flight, Jim stumbled from the car when they reached the restaurant. He was ushered into a private room, where he received greetings from ten or twelve men. He knew some of their names from working with them previously through email. Jim was then placed in the "seat of honor." That was when he learned, to his surprise, that all of these people were there for him. After a long dinner, with food that "was never meant for a stomach like mine" and too many drinks, the team produced a karaoke machine. After a few songs, Jim was invited to sing.

"I'll make a fool of myself," he told the only other Westerner in the room.

"That's the point," said the more culturally experienced expatriate.

The next morning, Jim received an early call from Cassandra. She wanted to be on time for their first day in the new office. She had requested that the driver pick them up at 7:30 a.m. Jim was ready on time, even though his head was aching from the previous night's "festivities." The host met them in the lobby of the hotel, dressed just as freshly as she had been the day before.

"Good morning, Ms. Hayes, Mr. Thorton," said the host.

"Please, call me Cassandra," Cassandra said again.

"Yes, Ms. Hayes," said the host. It was clear that Cassandra was not going to make any progress breaking down barriers with her.

When they reached the company campus, there were offices for both Cassandra and Jim, well prepared with supplies. There was coffee instead of tea and even flowers provided by the host. It was noticeable, however, that Jim's drinking companions were not there. They did not come in until midmorning, just in time to go to lunch with both Cassandra and Jim.

By late afternoon, it finally seemed that there was some momentum and productivity in the office. Cassandra and Jim attended separate meetings according to their responsibilities. Even with his energy dwindling, Jim fully participated in a critique of the current marketing effort. In fact, it seemed to Jim that he was the only one contributing, because the rest of the team sat silently as he tried to improve on the concept.

Thinking that they would go back to the hotel around 5:00 p.m., Cassandra and Jim tried to keep busy while waiting for the host, but she did not arrive until 7:00. Even then, the office was still buzzing. "Don't these people have families?" thought Cassandra. The same group of colleagues took Jim out again that night for food, bad drinks, and karaoke. He returned to the hotel just before midnight.

Culture in Real Time

Yongju, Cassandra, and Jim all thought they had prepared for their expat assignments, yet they were completely surprised by what they encountered upon arrival. In today's interconnected world, organizations and individuals regularly face the frustrations of distance, misunderstanding, inefficiency, and even outright failure in global teams. Culture is often at the root of these problems. In fact, cultural difference is the leading cause of conflict in global work teams, causing alienation and marginalization. These issues, in turn, can lead to a decrease in productivity and even to business-relationship breakups or noncompliance and legal problems.[2]

We all are deeply immersed in our own cultures, so much so that we don't even recognize it. Culture helps us to process a great deal of information quickly and to know how to act in a given situation. If we were forced to ponder each encounter of each day without precedent to rely on, human interaction would go into slow motion. We need to see things in patterns or categories that allow us to navigate complex social settings in real time. When we encounter conflict with another culture, those patterns and categories no longer work, and we react emotionally. Just like Yongju, Cassandra, and Jim, we get confused, frustrated, offended, or even angry.

Culture is a way of solving problems collectively. We learn these patterns of problem solving from our social environments at an early age. We learn the "right" way to interact with others, deal with conflict, build relationships, and so on. But as our social circles begin to expand, we see that others do things differently. We learn through our cultures how to know if something is true, but we see that others may have different ways of identifying truth. We learn through our cultures how to identify ourselves in collectives and communities, but we see that others identify themselves in different ways and in different communities. We learn in our cultures the value of time and relationships, but we see that others place different values on time and relationships. We have similar experiences in learning about social hierarchies, the impacts of emotion and rationality, and other key questions that have a strong effect on social, business, and political relationships.

There are three sets of practical questions that run through this book and are at the core of successfully navigating cultural gaps. The first set turns the focus on you. Answering these questions will help you understand yourself and your automatic behaviors and then be able to communicate that understanding to others:

- Who am I?
- What are my cultural values?
- How does my culture tell me to solve common problems?

The second set of questions is about others. Answering these questions will help you understand others and develop common language to describe your differences:

- Who are they?
- What do they value?
- How does their culture tell them to solve common problems?

The third and final set of questions is about you and others together. Answering these questions will help you create Culture3 Dialogue, a critical tool in building bridges among teammates from different cultures:

- What can we create together?
- How can we build a third, intercultural culture that will allow us to work together without giving up who we are?

Since the 1940s, Western researchers have been working to understand the fundamental differences between various cultures and how these differences impact the workforce in multinational companies. Researchers such as Edward T. Hall, Samuel A. Stouffer, Geert Hofstede, and Fons Trompenaars developed effective and useful methodologies used by IBM, American Express, and other global companies to help their multicultural teams to work more effectively together. However, even though these principles are used in top international business schools and global companies, this information hasn't made its way into common use and knowledge. It is also often presented in such a complex way that it takes days or weeks to begin to understand it. Our goal is to make this valuable information accessible, memorable, and easier to use.

This book is not about the complex aspects of culture or the subtle nuances that can lead to detailed philosophical differences. Nor is it about the protocols of when to kiss, bow, hug, or shake hands. Instead, this book will help managers and leaders more deeply understand themselves and the people they encounter and thereby help them learn how to build bridges together.

Let's get started.

CHAPTER 2
The Peach and the Coconut: Culture Made Simple

When multicultural teams are unable to work together effectively, the price of failure is high. In the story about Yongju, Cassandra, and Jim in chapter 1, hundreds of people participated in the same company-wide program. The strategy, however, achieved less-than-optimal results:

- Yongju became frustrated and eventually alienated. He changed jobs to work in an "all-Korean" firm.
- Jim turned down his next overseas assignment and moved into a part of the company that had less global interaction.
- Cassandra, however, tried to understand what had happened and eventually learned to better manage her relationships with Korean colleagues. Later, she was assigned to the company's European office, where she repeated her success. Today, she manages a major international division of the company.

As these employees' experiences show, cultural first encounters can be positive or negative. When they go badly, individuals become offended and frustrated, feeling that they are robbed of the opportunity to be productive. On a larger scale, the cost of lost opportunities for this company is staggering. If the stories of Yongju, Cassandra, and Jim are representative, two out of every three participants had a negative experience in the exchange program. Over time, the wounds from negative cultural encounters can heal, but much like the aftermath of a physical injury, emotional scar tissue develops, and people can become culturally less flexible.

Based on these experiences, culture might seem like a barrier that must be overcome in order for international teammates to be able to work together. But what if culture were viewed rather as an opportunity? What if cultural differences were a way to maximize personal growth, grow human potential, and gain competitive advantages in business? What if cultural differences were not conflicts but critical learning opportunities?

Some people survive the initial shock of a cultural first encounter and then feel their way through the maze of confusing cultural signals, but most people retreat to the familiar. That's what Yongju and Jim did. The informed and persistent, like Cassandra, eventually gain great personal, professional, social, and even political benefits. They forge lasting bonds with new friends and coworkers from many places, holding different values but sharing common purposes. When cultural transcendence is achieved, communication is improved, and wasteful conflict and errors are reduced.

Do you want to be like Yongju and Jim or like Cassandra? If your answer is "like Cassandra," read on.

Questions to Ask in a First Encounter

Cassandra asked herself three questions when she was confronted with cultural differences. These questions are asked in every successful cultural encounter (whether first or subsequent). While they are simple, they also feel risky and even dangerous in real time. But if asked, they can make the difference between having a positive, growth-starting cultural encounter and having a negative, emotionally scarring one.

First, rather than focusing on how others were different from her, Cassandra focused inward. She asked herself, "What do these people see when they see me?" The importance of this question cannot be over-stated. When you begin a cultural encounter with a question to yourself, you are taking an unusual stance. That is, unlike most people in the same situation, you are *not* assuming that "they" (members of the other culture) are wrong and "we" (members of your culture) are right. Instead, you are assuming responsibility for the success of the encounter. By asking and answering this question, you can determine how you can share your core beliefs and values without being prescriptive or demanding.

Once you have examined yourself, then and only then can you look at the other person or people in the encounter. The second question asks, "What do I see when I see you?" or, in other words, "How are you different from me?" This question is much more than an inquiry about food or greeting customs. Rather, this question asks something profound about others' beliefs and core values.

The third question examines how international groups can cooperate. It asks, "What common ground can we stand on together?" There is nothing more binding and rewarding than being productive with another person. By asking this question, you begin to discover how people from different cultures can learn together, build a friendship, create a business, or solve a problem. Cassandra said, "Sometimes it's pretty hard, but I realized very early that the short-term awkwardness of a first encounter could yield long-term benefits for me and for my new colleague. We both just needed to take those first steps towards each other, expose ourselves to a little risk, and then learn to walk together."

How to See Yourself and Others

Most of this book (chapters 3–10) is about the answers to the first two questions. Chapter 11 is about strategies for building common ground with Culture3 Dialogue. We (the authors) know from our years of experience working with students, executives, diplomats, and military personnel that an essential step in building a cultural bridge is having a clear, simple mental map of one's own cultural values and beliefs.

This is where a simple metaphor known as the Peach and Coconut Concept can help you understand yourself and others. Once you grasp this concept, it can be used as a mirror on your own culture and as a lens through which to see other cultures. While the Peach and Coconut Concept is based on complex research on cultural differences, it simplifies that information for the sake of easy access and a quick start. If you want to dig into the details behind the concept, see the bibliography for a number of excellent books about cultural differences. If you are ready to dive into mastering cultural first encounters and learning how to build productive relationships with people who are different, read on.

Two Types of Culture

The cultures of the world can be simplified into two basic groups: Peach cultures and Coconut cultures.

Peach cultures are easy to access, just as a peach has a thin skin covering its sweet fruit. Connections are easily made and easily broken. Friendship comes with little effort, and there is willingness to share. But at the core of the culture, like the pit of a peach, people are private and hard. There are topics that are not discussed, even with those who are closest to a person. Peaches (members of Peach cultures) have many friends at the fruit level but few at the pit level. Additionally, Peach cultures focus on what is best for society overall. They prize fairness and a level playing field. Time follows an agenda; life is compartmentalized; and one's place in society is based on one's own efforts and achievement. Peach cultures also have, as you will see later, a lot of rules that apply to everyone equally. If relationships come into conflict with rules or a sense of fairness, the rules will win out. The United States (US), the United Kingdom (UK), Germany, and many northern European countries have Peach cultures.

In Coconut cultures, there is a hard outer shell that does not allow newcomers to join easily. One must demonstrate a degree of loyalty to the group in order to be allowed in. The thickness of the shell and the methods for penetrating it may vary among Coconut cultures, but they all have one thing in common: one must be patient and willing to spend time developing trusting relationships in a variety of settings, both personal and professional. In fact, the focus of Coconut cultures is on relationships and the good of the group. Rules, time, and boundaries all bend in the service of these relationships. First encounters with Coconuts (members of Coconut cultures) may seem difficult or impossible, but persistence and patience will reap a great reward: friends for life who will go to great lengths for one another. Once you have been accepted into the heart of a Coconut, you can go anywhere. Nothing is off limits. Most countries in Asia, Latin America, Africa, and the Middle East, along with a few countries in Europe, have Coconut cultures.

Of course, there is a spectrum of cultures, ranging from extreme Peach to extreme Coconut (see **Figure 1**). Even within the same culture, some people may be more Peach-like while others are more Coconut-like. There will even be some people who overlap from one culture into another. Culture is nuanced and complex; there is plenty of depth for those who want to explore it. But the simplicity of the Peach and Coconut Concept is immediately useful and provides a helpful gateway to beginning the process of overcoming cultural differences.

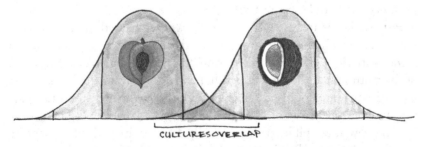

CULTURES OVERLAP

Figure 1. The double bell curve for Peach cultures and
Coconut cultures. Notice the overlapping sections.

Are You a Peach or a Coconut?

As you continue reading this book, try to be objective about yourself and how you may fit into one or both culture types. It can be difficult to see how we are influenced by our own cultures, but allow yourself to look at your behaviors from another perspective. In a way, we (the authors) are asking you to step out of your own skin. If you can, even to a small degree, you will start to see that some ideas and attitudes that you thought were absolutes actually come from your culture and are seen and valued differently by others.

One of the objectives of this book is to help you and the members of your team transcend your various cultures and develop Culture3 Dialogue, a tool that will help you create a new workplace culture in which all team members feel valued and respected so that they can work together to effectively meet goals. We hope to help you gain a clearer understanding of yourself, develop the vocabulary necessary to discuss differences in cultural values, and learn to work with others more effectively. The first steps in this process are to understand the culture you come from and to accept that the values others hold are as valid as those which may seem absolute, unchangeable, and "right" to you.

PEACH CULTURES

Peach cultures focus on the individual, with priority on rules, truth, or a sense of fairness. Peaches are easy to get to know, but there is a limit to what they are willing to do for a friend. There are lots of rules that apply to everyone equally. Time follows an agenda, life is compartmentalized, and one's place in society is based on achievement.

COCONUT CULTURES

Coconut cultures focus on relationships. Loyalty to the group is the priority and is the basis for security and trust. It is not easy to get through the outer shell, but inside are lifelong friends who will go to great lengths for each other. Rules, time, and boundaries all bend in the service of relationships.

Participate in discussions on social media:
#Peach&Coconut #PeachCulture #CoconutCulture

A Glimpse into a Peach Culture

Cassandra Hayes and Jim Thorton come from the US, a Peach culture in which fairness and equality are valued. US culture revolves around providing unbiased information to help an individual or organization make the optimal decision for any given situation. Relationships are established (and sometimes detached) easily because everyone is playing by a set of shared rules. When relationships interfere with the pursuit of fairness and an optimal outcome, those relationships are seen as questionable, harmful, or even illegal. People are on the watch for nepotism, and efforts are made to root it out.

To maintain this level playing field, US society has a lot of rules that apply to everyone equally. This mindset appears in families, organizations, and the country in general. Contracts and the rule of law arise from this system of values. This is where the pit of the US Peach comes in: in general, it is not acceptable to breach this ideal of fairness to help a friend or even a close family member.

In US culture, the way one interacts with one's team is largely egalitarian and based on merit. In a group discussion, everyone is expected to contribute, regardless of his or her status. Ideas that contribute to solving a problem are highly valued, and it doesn't matter who raises these ideas. The best idea may come from the department coordinator; if so, that's the idea the team will use. When a team needs to choose a new member, a candidate's past accomplishments tend to weigh more heavily than his or her social connections. This way, the team will hopefully hire the person with the best ability to do the job.

Note that these paragraphs describe the ideal in US culture; it doesn't always work this way. But in pursuit of these principles, more rules and processes are put in place to get closer to the ideal.

A Glimpse into a Coconut Culture

Yongju Lee comes from Korea, a Coconut culture where everything revolves around relationships. Why was it such a shock for him that he had to find his own way to the hotel from the airport? Why was it hurtful that his arrival seemed like a complete surprise? Why was he so angry about the marketing discussion when he had remained silent throughout the conversation?

Up to this point in his life, Yongju had always been a member of a close-knit group with a clearly defined hierarchy. In Korean culture, older people and senior staff are treated with explicit respect, and other team members look to them for guidance and direction. Loyalty to leaders and the group is of utmost importance. Everyone in a given group, regardless of his or her position on the social ladder, has obligations to the other group members.

In Coconut cultures, one does not join a group easily. There is an outer shell around it that protects lifelong relationships. To be allowed inside, a newcomer must be proven and tested. It takes time to carefully and gently earn the trust that gradually draws one into the group. Because of the depth of relationships and the need to understand how others will behave in a variety of situations, there are really no boundaries between work and personal life. People who work together often socialize on evenings and weekends. Long lunches are critically important in the development and nurturing of these relationships.

The bonds inside the group also act to reduce the risk of agreements falling apart over time. In Peach cultures, contracts are used for this purpose, but in Coconut cultures, contracts do not mean as much. It is the warmth and reciprocal obligations of the network of relationships that provide stability and mitigate risk.

Most of the world's cultures are some variation on the Coconut theme, and some cultures have their own name for it. For example, Chinese speakers use the word *guanxi* (广西), which can be roughly translated as "relationship" or "network of reciprocal obligations" and has much more depth of meaning than the English word *relationship*. Similarly, some refer to French culture as "the baguette" after the French bread of the same name, which has a hard crust and a soft interior. In social science, the terms *in-group* and *collectivist* are used. Regardless of names or nuances, it is important for both Coconuts and Peaches to understand how Coconut cultures function.

A Glimpse into the Third Option

While the Peach and Coconut Concept is helpful, it only goes so far. Later in this book, we have included a series of country reports that help you see whether a particular country's culture aligns with Peach patterns or Coconut patterns. But some countries do not match completely with one type or the other. Several of the listed countries have some cultural dimensions that align with Peach values and some that align with Coconut values.

At an individual level, you will also see people who are a mix of Peach and Coconut. Such people may have grown up in mixed families, with one Peach parent and one Coconut parent. Or they may have spent part of their upbringing in one culture and then moved to another. Some people are also able to acquire skills from both types of cultures because of professional development. When we presented this model to a group of diplomats, one man who had been living outside his own culture for most of his life said, "I'm a CocoPeach." This simple description captures the complexity of people who are living bridges between cultures.

COCOPEACH

A CocoPeach is someone who is multicultural. He or she has grown up between two cultures or otherwise acquired native-level patterns of behavior from both. In most cases, however, one should not expect to develop native-level sensibilities from another culture later in life. Participate in discussions on social media:

#CocoPeach

In the next chapter, we will introduce seven dimensions of culture that help us begin to distinguish between Peach and Coconut cultures. As you study this layer of complexity, you will begin to see how day-to-day, minute-to-minute behaviors reflect cultural values. The questions associated with each dimension are related to some of a culture's most basic values, such as time, relationships, and status. These questions will help you to realize how others see you, to understand people who are different, and to begin building bridges that will transcend those differences.

Establishing Culture3 Dialogue

If you identify your own cultural preferences using the self-assessments in the next several chapters, then you will have a good idea where you fall in within the Peach and Coconut Concept. This self-identification is only the first step on your journey, but it is a big one. Once you see yourself, you can start understanding how others see you.

This understanding leads to the second step on your journey: identifying what others are. For instance, if you prefer organized meetings that start on time, then you are likely monochronic. Others on your team may prefer more-open and less-restrictive meetings; they are likely polychronic (you will learn more about these terms in chapter 7). So how do you have productive meetings that use the best of both your way and your teammates' way?

In this situation, the average person says that the team should use "my" way because the teammates' way is "not appropriate," "not efficient," or "bad" in some way. When we take this approach, we impose our way on others. But a more productive and sustainable strategy is to take the third step on the journey and work towards another way of doing things—not "my" way, not "their" way, but "our" way. We call this technique establishing Culture3 Dialogue. Each chapter contains suggestions for how to establish Culture3 Dialogue so that your team can work together effectively and reach its goals and beyond.

CHAPTER 3
The Seven Questions of Culture

Mangus was a white South African of Dutch descent. Despite living in a post-apartheid country, he had seen more division than unity in his life. Blacks and poor people were kept on one side of the "wall," and rich white people lived on the other side. There were strict rules that governed the relationships between the cultures on either side of the "wall." But Mangus was also friendly and kind. He loved making new friends and being in new places. Still, when he got off the airplane to attend college in the US—his first time outside his country—he was shocked to see people with many shades of skin standing in line together in front of him.

Later, Mangus met his dormitory roommate, Marcos. Marcos was a first-generation Hispanic immigrant to the US. His family lived near campus, and his father worked two jobs to keep Marcos in school. Marcos was close to his family and was often described as "the life of the party."

The two young men began their relationship with conflict and difficulty that they later learned to transcend. Each roommate describes this process in his own words:[3]

Mangus

When I first checked into the dormitory, I was glad to see that there were some very clear rules about what we could and could not do. I had worked long and hard to get into the university, and I didn't want it to go down the drain because someone was out of control. It was nice to see that 10 p.m. was the start of quiet time and that lights-out was at 11 p.m.

I was a little bit surprised when I met my roommate, Marcos. He seemed like a nice guy, but he was the first Hispanic person I'd ever met, and I wondered if he was like the people of Indian descent whom I had encountered in South Africa. I didn't have a problem being around people who were black or brown, even though a lot of people assumed I was a racist because I was white and had been born in South Africa.

Our first conflict came when I realized that the start of quiet time at 10 p.m. was almost completely ignored, not just by Marcos but also by everybody else in the dormitory. Most of them were talking to their girlfriends on the phone or making plans for the weekend, and they just didn't seem to care what time it was. I figured that their lights would go out at 11 p.m., but that didn't happen either. When I complained, everyone just laughed. I was annoyed because I wanted to get up early the next morning and do my homework. I was also surprised the next day when I came home and found somebody working on my computer. The person just said, "I thought you wouldn't mind."

Marcos

School was going great except for my roommate. He was really strict on the rules, almost military-like. He also never smiled and didn't seem very interested in my family or me. I thought he was going to freak out when we didn't quiet down after 10 p.m. I mean, who really takes that seriously? The rest of us stayed up until after midnight getting to know each other. After all, we were going to spend the next year together. Mangus kept trying to go to sleep. Sort of strange.

I got up early, just like him, but came home in the quiet of the afternoon and took a nap. We were planning a big floor party for the dorm over the weekend, and I thought I'd be up pretty late with the guys. Mangus did not seem interested. Also, my family was having a party for me that weekend. I was thinking about inviting him, but I had second thoughts because I thought he would feel awkward.

Bridging the (Roommate) Chasm

It seems there could not be a bigger cultural divide between these two young men. Mangus was focused on his individual performance in college; Marcos wanted to make friends and build a community. Mangus wanted rules to bring familiar structure; Marcos wanted to be part of a group. Mangus respected the authority of the dorm residents; Marcos saw them as peers. Mangus was always on time; Marcos took time to include everyone. Mangus was "appropriate;" Marcos was "affectionate." Mangus was specific about his wants and needs; Marcos was "good with pretty much anything."

When the roommates finally had a meeting to work things out, Marcos was emotional, while Mangus was rational and passive. In fact, it took three all-night talks, a shoving match, and a couple of failed double dates, but eventually these two young men became lifelong friends.

In this chapter, we expand on the Peach and Coconut Concept to provide another set of tools for people like Mangus and Marcos. These tools go beyond the Peach and the Coconut symbols to provide deeper access to cultural understanding.

Some say that culture cannot be seen, touched, or even accurately measured. It is symbolic, with ghostlike qualities. But even if we cannot see this "ghost," it has a significant impact on our lives. It drives behaviors that are observable, and those behaviors have real consequences. Our view is that culture is best understood not through people's *explanations* of their cultures but through observable *behaviors*. We must be able to observe a construction like culture in order to measure it, understand it, and adapt our own behavior to it. Otherwise, culture would be such a subjective concept that no one could sufficiently agree on what it is, so no one could make any claims about it either.

So in this search for cultural understanding, what sorts of behaviors should we consider? Protocol, while important, is not really a measure of culture. When to kiss, bow, shake hands, hug, and so on is important but is not a measure of culture. To be a measure of culture, a behavior must be motivated by social problem solving. It must be a learned behavior that addresses an important issue for society. In other words, it must address a grand problem—not a "What shall we have for dinner tonight?" kind of problem but a "What is truth and how can I know it?" kind of problem.

In this chapter and the ensuing chapters, we examine seven key dimensions of culture that address grand, important, and often invisible issues. At their core, these dimensions explain the nature of truth, the value of time, the creation of identity and social status, and other key concepts that appear in every culture on the planet. Research about these dimensions has been ongoing since the 1960s. Unfortunately, this treasure trove of information makes the process of studying culture prohibitively complex for global-business managers who do not have the time to become cultural anthropologists.

We have framed the seven dimensions as the Seven Questions of Culture, a series of queries that could be posed to an individual within a culture. Each question is associated with an important social construct, such as time, truth, identity, hierarchy, etc. The response to each question can be placed on a spectrum to show how closely that response aligns with Peach or Coconut cultural values. The Seven Questions and their associated spectrums are outlined below and will be further detailed in chapters 4–10.

The Seven Questions of Culture

1. How do we define our identity?
2. How do we find what is true?
3. How do we work together as a team?
4. How do we deal with time?
5. How do we deal with status?
6. How do we approach our work?
7. What is our emotional style?

Figure 2 shows the spectrum of cultural values that is associated with each of the Seven Questions.

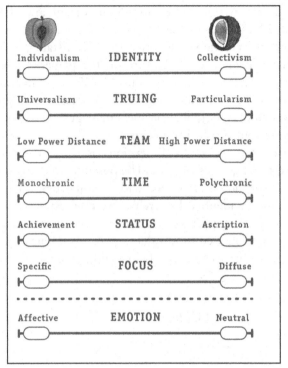

Figure 2. The seven cultural dimensions and their associated spectrums of cultural values.

The next several paragraphs provide an overview of the Seven Questions. Each question will be explored in detail later in this book.

1. How do we define our identity? (chapter 4)

- Is individual performance or team performance more valued?
- What is the range of rewards from low performers to high performers?
- What happens when individuals "stick out?"

Universalism   **TRUING**   Particularism

2. How do we find what is true? (chapter 5)

- What is the role of rules in society, and how important are they?
- How much flexibility is granted in following rules?
- What is the role of relationships in society?
- Who decides what it means to "do the right thing"?

Low Power Distance   **TEAM**   High Power Distance

3. How do we work together as a team? (chapter 6)

- How is team membership determined?
- How equal are team members?
- How are conflicts resolved?
- How are work processes determined?

Monochronic   **TIME**   Polychronic

4. How do we deal with time? (chapter 7)

- Is time linear or cyclical?
- How past-/present-/future-oriented are we?
- How do we conduct meetings?
- What do we consider to be a deadline?
- How do we hold each other accountable for meeting deadlines?

Achievement **STATUS** **Ascription**

5. How do we deal with status? (chapter 8)

- Who is granted status?
- How is status earned?
- What is the social distance between high-status and low-status individuals?

Specific **FOCUS** **Diffuse**

6. How do we approach our work? (chapter 9)

- Do we start with the context or with a specific point?
- Do we view projects from a wide angle or from a close-up?
- Is work integrated with or separate from our personal lives?

Affective **EMOTION** **Neutral**

7. What is our emotional style?

- How are emotions displayed?
- What is our verbal style?
- What is the value of rationalism?
- How are different ideas given weight?

Rules or Relationships?

So if you are reading for speed, remember this: Peaches, like Mangus, prefer rules. Coconuts, like Marcos, prefer relationships. This does not mean that Peaches don't care about relationships or that Coconuts don't care about rules. It means that in a forced choice, a Peach will follow rules even if doing so hurts relationships, while a Coconut will violate rules to preserve relationships.

You are beginning to see how complicated it can be to tell the difference between Peach culture and Coconut culture. Remember that with a Peach, there is soft flesh just below the skin and a pit in the center. It is relatively easy to be accepted among Peaches. With a Coconut, there is a hard shell around the outside, but the inside is sweet to the center. However, one must take great care and allow time to develop relationships in order to be invited past the shell; it cannot be quickly or forcibly cracked. Anyone who is in a hurry or reacts angrily to differences in values will cause the shell to harden and will not be admitted to a Coconut group.

In general terms, Peaches see identity as an individual matter. Like Cassandra Hayes (see chapter 1), they are secure on their own, easy to get to know, informal, and largely unworried about belonging to a group. When joining a new team, a Peach brings with him or her a set of standards and work habits that are fixed. While Cassandra likes her coworkers and is loyal to them, her first loyalty is to the rules of the organization. She gets to work on time, works defined hours, and works in specific ways and to set standards.

Yongju Lee (see chapter 1), however, defines his identity in terms of the group or groups he belongs to. Because he has invested in his work relationships throughout his career, it is very stressful for him to break from an established workgroup and join another. When he does, he expects a ritualistic welcome that will help him break through the new group's outer shell. As a result, he needs a lot of attention to help him feel welcome and valued. For Yongju, rules are less important than relationships. He will break or bend rules to protect the relationships he values. Yongju is a Coconut.

Can One Metaphor Really Explain All Cultures?

The Peach and Coconut concept of culture is quite different from other ways of defining culture. Various ethnicities, religions, genders, or geographical locations are often said to have their own cultures. However, by setting aside these common ideas and focusing on behaviors and values, we can obtain richer insights and make better predictions about how members of a given culture are likely to behave. For example, one can make a case that the Irish have a strong culture. It attracts about three million tourists to Ireland every year. But while there are about ten million Irish living in Ireland, there are about seventy million people worldwide who identify as Irish. Thus, geography is an inadequate way of defining Irish culture because that culture is really found all over the world.

As another example, the UK was once largely a racially white society of Celts, Anglo-Saxons, and other groups that historically inhabited the British Isles. Thanks to deep traditions in literature and philosophy, the evolution of English culture is well documented. But in recent decades, many people have left former British colonies and moved to England. Now a new generation of racially mixed, African-, South Asian–, and Middle Eastern–looking people speak with an English accent and quote Shakespeare.

In summary, race, gender, tribe, religion, geography, and other traditional markers do not reveal all you need to know about a person's cultural values. To build the understanding needed to create Culture3 Dialogue, you first need to apply the Seven Questions of Culture to yourself and your teammates. Then you need to observe your own behaviors and those of your teammates to collect the data needed to answer the questions.

Caution: Avoid Stereotyping

As you seek cultural understanding, you must look beyond the surface to see how groups and individuals solve problems using culture. But do not project onto others things that might not be there. A person's values and behaviors are not determined solely by the culture from which he or she comes.

As an illustration, think back to the double bell curve of Peach and Coconut cultures (see **Figure 1** in chapter 2). If you were to answer the Seven Questions of Culture for two vastly different countries, you would find stark contrasts but also certain features in common. For example, the US is often identified as having an individualist culture. Japan, on the other hand, is often identified as having a collectivist culture. The completed double bell curve shows that many of the data points for these two countries are nowhere near each other. But the edges of the curves overlap, indicating that there are some Japanese people who are individualist and some in the US who are collectivist.

In other words, the ability to make general statements about cultures, while useful, does not allow us to make specific statements about individuals. We can get into a lot of trouble by assuming that an individual from a particular culture perfectly matches a generalized statement about that culture. If we take cultural generalizations too seriously, we risk offending individuals who are unusual or unique within their own cultures. Here are some examples of such people:

- Individualists in China, which is a largely collectivist culture
- Collectivists in Australia, which is a largely individualist culture
- Achievement-oriented people in the UK, which is largely an ascription-oriented culture (in which people are born into and assigned their positions in society)
- Ascription-oriented people in the US, which is largely an achievement-oriented culture (in which one's position in society is determined by what one has accomplished)

To provide starting points on your journey to Culture3 Dialogue, chapters 4–10 do contain cultural generalizations based on the Seven Questions of Culture. Again, these generalizations are useful but do not necessarily apply to every individual within a particular culture. Each chapter follows this outline:

- Overview of one of the Seven Questions
- Descriptions of the cultural traits that answer that question
- One or more case studies of those cultural traits
- Self-assessment
- Using the question to establish Culture3 Dialogue

CHAPTER 4
How Do We Define Our Identity?

 **IDENTITY**

Individualism   Collectivism

Question 1: How do we define our identity?

- Is individual performance or team performance more valued?
- What is the range of rewards from low performers to high performers?
- What happens when individuals "stick out?"

Kumar was the best employee in a small plant in India. He was not the plant manager, but he was "the glue that holds the factory together," according to almost all of his colleagues and superiors. He knew the factory's processes, understood its finances, and knew most of the people in the plant as they largely came from the same village.

Each year, members of the plant's parent company visited from the UK. During these visits, Kumar did most of the hosting, did most of the talking, and got most of the credit. Several times the parent company had offered to make him the manager of another plant in India, with appropriate salary raises and benefits, but he had always declined. Yet, to the surprise of human-resources personnel at company headquarters, Kumar was not highly evaluated by his superiors. He was criticized for "not being a team player" and "being too ambitious."

In 2008, during the global financial crisis, the production of the plant was reduced by fifty percent, and it was decided that the workforce needed to be reduced by about thirty percent. A list of employees to be laid off was circulated among middle managers. In a meeting to finalize the list, Kumar asked why he was not being laid off. "I am not a team player," he confessed sadly to the group. "My father says I shine before my time. And I am the youngest manager from my village in the factory. I don't want to come to work if I have to pass the home of my elder who has lost his job. I would rather it be me."

He was strongly collectivist. For Kumar, his group roles and his relationships with his neighbors were much more important than his job, individual performance, or reputation. He was laid off and quickly hired by a competing company in a neighboring village.

Our lives are construction projects in which we build our identities one brick at a time. The bricks of our identities are our words, dress, values, behavior, and culture. US writer Norman Maclean, author of *A River Runs Through It*, said that the symbolic construction of identity is not just an important thing; it is the only thing that we do.

So how does someone go about the lifetime project of creating an identity? Interestingly, a culture's answer to this question of identity often (but not always) predicts its answers to the other questions and thus what type of culture it is. If a culture scores as strongly individualist, it is probably a Peach culture. If a culture scores as strongly collectivist, it is probably a Coconut culture.

Individualist Peaches versus Collectivist Coconuts

The difference between individualist cultures and collectivist cultures is the most important concept in this book. Individualist cultures focus on the rules that govern the interactions between people. Individual difference is identified, named, and celebrated. In collectivist cultures, identity is defined by the group, and the emphasis is on the relationships between group members. Individuals who stick out are seen as "bad sports" on athletic teams or "not team players" at work. These opposite values have enormous effects on how Peach and Coconut cultures define identity.

For most Peaches, the project of identity building depends mostly on oneself. Peaches create individual résumés, vitae, or report cards. At school, they wear unique clothing to express themselves, and they play on sports teams but keep track of their personal statistics, meaning that even in a team setting, individuals can stand out and stand above others. They earn individual awards and diplomas and place them on walls for others to see. In short, Peaches are individualists.

Unlike Peaches, Coconuts grow better in bunches. They begin building their identities by learning about their communities, groups, families, or classes. They work hard to fit in. At school, they wear uniforms, play team sports, and win team trophies. They form deep, often-lifelong relationships with their school peers. They honor teachers, parents, grandparents, and others who have been the guardians of their communities for generations. In short, Coconuts are collectivists.

Peaches must see themselves as differentiated from others. Because everyone is so different, rules are crucial to show how to manage the complex interactions between people. Coconuts do not want to be differentiated. They want to be seen as the same as everyone else in their families, tribes, neighborhoods, work teams, or other groups.

In predominantly individualistic cultures, it is generally believed that the quality of life is enhanced through the efforts of the individual and that society as a whole benefits from the contributions and creativity of each unique person. Society expects individuals to make their own decisions and to be responsible only for themselves and perhaps their immediate families. People tend to measure their own actions against internal personal standards. Therefore, individual freedom and personal development are highly prized.

In predominantly collectivist cultures, most people believe that the quality of life is enhanced through individual commitment to group goals and norms. Everyone benefits from social harmony, so a balance is struck: the group provides help and protection in exchange for obedience and loyalty from individuals. People's actions are measured against common standards of behavior that support social harmony. Therefore, social training and group approval are highly prized.

Peach Case Study: The US

The US clearly has an individualist culture. The quintessential "American hero" is the cowboy: a rugged loner whose deep values, strong work ethic, and willingness to take risks make him a champion. The cowboy takes on the bad guys against all odds. He confronts evil head-on, without compromise, and brings justice to the weak and the weary. Cowboys, at least as depicted by Hollywood, seldom ride in a group or look to the group in defining what is right and what is wrong.

The history of the US is often written as a collection of individual efforts by exceptional individuals. As if studying the characters in a play, they learn about Thomas Jefferson, Patrick Henry, George Washington, and other individuals who played a key role in the formation of their nation. When studying the expansion of the Old West, one reads about Davy Crockett, Jed Smith, Jim Bridger, Brigham Young, and other individuals who opened the frontier. US history emphasizes the greatness of larger-than-life heroes and quickly overlooks the less-prominent contributions of the ordinary soldier, citizen, or follower.

The images of cowboys and the Founding Fathers are alive and well in the minds of US business managers. While collaboration skills are often widely advertised for, most managers highly value the ability of an individual to lead the pack. Performance appraisals and career planning in US corporations are largely used to support individual accomplishment. For example, it is impossible to get a job in the US without producing a résumé. The résumé generally contains a list of individual accomplishments that include college degrees, work successes, and experience. It is not uncommon for US businesspeople to change jobs quite frequently, using their résumés and work experience to propel them from job to job and from workgroup to workgroup. Standing out as a strong individual is a desirable trait in US corporations.

Coconut Case Study: Japan

To understand collectivism, it is important to understand the concept of *guanxi* (first referred to in chapter 2), which comes from China but is applicable to collectivist cultures in general. *Guanxi* captures the idea that in collective societies, careful rules apply to group insiders and outsiders and describe how each person is to be treated. People in collectivist societies tend to identify more with a group than they do with their own individual accomplishments. This kind of identification is so deeply rooted that it often shows up in language.

For instance, those learning Japanese are taught to say "I go to the university" by using this phrase: "*Watackishi wa dai gaku ni ekimasu.*" Translated literally, it means "I to university go." This construction makes perfect sense to a Japanese-learning foreigner who comes from an individualist culture. But native Japanese speakers don't typically use this phrase. Instead, they say "*Dai gaku ni ekimasu,*" which means "Go to university"; the "I" is implied. Thus, this same phrase could mean "We go to the university" or "I go to the university." In Japanese, it's not important to distinguish who is doing it. This notion of collectivism pours out across the entire Japanese culture.

For example, when it came time for a plant manager in Japan to retire, he wanted to still be useful to the company and be in contact with his friends. So he took a job driving the company bus. Every day, he would get up early in the morning, drive the bus to an apartment building, and take several loads of workers to the factory. Every night, he would return the workers to their living quarters. In Peach cultures, it would be difficult to imagine a retired plant manager providing this kind of service to former colleagues. But in Japan, harmony and fellowship are highly valued. Serving the collective good is the ultimate goal.

For a collectivist culture, standing out as an individual is not a desired trait. A common saying to describe such cultures is "The nail that sticks up gets hammered down." Some Japanese scientists, for example, have not received credit for individual inventions or discoveries because their teams are given credit first. Group harmony and collective accomplishment is much more important in Japanese culture than individual accomplishment.

Comparative Case Study: Japanese and US Baseball

To further explore the contrasts between Peach and Coconut cultures, it is useful to look at a sport beloved in both Japan and the US: professional baseball.

A number of baseball players have left the Japanese league to play in the US. While they are generally seen as heroes in Japan because they made the Pacific crossing to play in the best baseball league in the world, they are also viewed as traitors. Ichiro Suzuki, for example, who now plays for the Miami Marlins, is beloved by baseball fans in Japan. Over his career in the US, he has had ten consecutive two-hundred-hit seasons, the longest streak by any player in Major League Baseball history. In the US, it is assumed that he will eventually be inducted into the Baseball Hall of Fame. But Ichiro left a successful team in Japan to come to the US. Instead of just bidding him farewell, many Japanese people still see Ichiro's departure as a betrayal to his Japanese team. In their minds, he did not fulfill his duty to those who gave him a good start. Standing out as a great player in the US is considered less valuable than helping his team in Japan.

In fact, the entire baseball experience is completely different for both players and fans in these two cultures. Japanese players tend to be much more team oriented than US players, with many more sacrifices in hitting and base running. Teams as a whole are very popular in Japan, while individual players take a secondary role. But in the US, the player is the main object of interest, and the team is largely secondary. Japanese stadiums encourage vendors for opposing teams to attend and sell their merchandise. There are dedicated sections for opposing teams' fans, who try to out-cheer their rivals. Fans of both teams wear team colors, bring their own cheerleaders, and bond together in rituals that emphasize the tribal nature of fandom. But in the US, fans watch baseball as individuals even if they attend games in groups. They may or may not wear team colors. Some fans keep statistics during the game, others talk, and still others cheer or holler at the umpires.

Other Case Studies

Here are several other examples that contrast Peach (individualist) and Coconut (collectivist) behaviors:

- In a parade for a championship sports team in the US, the winner of the most valuable player (MVP) award was given a special seat on the team's float. The other players were honored, but she was revered. In a similar parade in China, the entire team sat together on the float. Their accomplishment in victory was shared equally.
- In one Australian corporation, employees' performance awards are proudly displayed around the office. The top-sales award is the most coveted. It comes with a bonus, a corner office, a marked parking place, and access to the executive cafeteria. In the same firm's Korean office, all workspaces are the same size, and everyone eats in the same cafeteria.
- In the US, government and educational buildings are named after "great people" (mostly men) who have done "great things." Statues of heroic individuals are erected outside such buildings, and portraits of past leaders hang in the public spaces inside. By the entries hang bronze plaques with the names of those who approved the construction of the buildings. In collectivist cultures, buildings are named after movements, events, or ideas. For instance, China's most important government building is

known as the Great Hall of the People. The focus is on things accomplished in groups.

Individualists and Collectivists in Business

Clearly, these vast differences in defining identity can lead to conflict between individualist and collectivist cultures. In the world of business, these difficulties most often arise in four areas: negotiations, decision-making, teamwork, and leadership priorities. By understanding these common struggles, you can be better prepared to navigate them when working with people from other cultures.

Negotiations

Negotiations can be particularly frustrating for businesspeople from opposite types of culture. Typically in Peach cultures, one person is authorized to negotiate and make commitments for his or her organization. But Coconut negotiators tend to come to the table in groups. They may make tentative agreements and withdraw to consult with their superiors. To Peaches, Coconuts may seem slow and noncommittal. To Coconuts, Peaches may seem hasty and demanding.

To minimize frustrations, keep these patterns in mind when negotiating with people from the opposite culture type. A Peach negotiator has authority to make and accept an offer. A Coconut negotiating team needs to discuss and "go talk to the sales manager" (or to whomever) before committing to an agreement.

Decision-Making

Decision-making is handled differently in Peach and Coconut cultures. In Peach cultures, a lone person is expected to make decisions within his or her organizational stewardship. It is often seen as a sign of weakness if that person consults with others. But in Coconut cultures, conferring and consulting with others demonstrates respect for their status. Often, Coconuts will spend an excessive (from the Peach point of view) amount of time working through an issue as a group before a decision is made. In other words, Peaches tend to be more decisive, while Coconuts tend to be more patient, consultative, and deliberative. Looked at more broadly, Peaches may speak for their organizations in decisive ways during negotiations, but upon returning to their organizations, they still need to build consensus around the final decision prior to implementation. To Coconuts, on the other hand, building consensus within their organizations is an important part of negotiations, so when agreement about final terms is reached, their organizations can move immediately to implementation.

Teamwork

Business-related teamwork is starkly different in Peach and Coconut cultures. In Peach cultures, teammates often split up the work of projects, assign individuals to complete each piece, and combine the pieces to create the final product. Teams are frequently broken up and re-formed, so it is normal for Peaches to serve on many teams with many different people during their careers. Most Peaches, however, have little to no contact with their teammates outside of work. On the other hand, Coconut cultures see teams as an important constant in both work and social life. Japan, for example, has mastered the art of creating constructive work teams. Teams are nurtured and used continuously to improve efficiency and product quality. Teammates work together on particular projects for many years, and their families might live next door to each other. Work teams often socialize after work, and the company often pays for the socialization activities. Managers have large expense accounts to entertain clients and coworkers.

Leadership Priorities

Peach leaders and Coconut leaders have different priorities. The traditional organization chart is an artifact of an individualist culture. In these organizations it is important to see which individuals lead which groups. They gain credibility by meeting organizational needs first. But in a Coconut culture, the first priority for managers is to create harmony within their teams or workgroups. Once this harmony is established, organizational needs can be addressed.

Self-Assessment: Individualist or Collectivist?

By now, you may be getting a sense of whether you are an individualist or a collectivist. To determine your category more specifically, fill out the table below by circling the option from each pair that best describes your preference *most of the time*. The results are nonscientific, but they are sufficient to trigger the self-examination required to establish Culture3 Dialogue.

Another way to utilize these self-assessments is to have each member of your team complete them and then talk about the results together. Discussing all the assessments in one meeting would be overwhelming, but looking at one or two at a time and talking about everyone's preferences can be a nonthreatening exercise in establishing Culture3 Dialogue together.

Individualism **IDENTITY** Collectivism

I prefer . . .	
Change that happens through individual creativity	An unchanging system
To take charge	To consult my colleagues
To stick out	To fit in
Personal goals	Group goals
Individual recognition and awards	Group recognition and awards
Making decisions individually	Building group consensus
An individual résumé or vita	A group work history
Personal standards	Group norms
Organizational hierarchy	Inclusion
Individual creativity	Group collaboration

If you circled more answers in the left column, you are likely a Peach (individualist). If you circled more answers in the right column, you are likely a Coconut (collectivist).

Now that you understand how you define your identity, let's explore how to overcome potential cultural conflicts when working with people who build their identities differently than you do.

Establishing Culture3 Dialogue

If you are a Peach working with Coconuts, take time to build relationships before getting down to business. Touting individual career accomplishments or degrees is not wise or productive. In meetings, honor the existing social order and hierarchy rather than trying to impose your hierarchy on the host organization. Be patient and learn the host organization's work history and processes. Remember that in a Coconut organization, decisions are typically made subtly and with consensus over time rather than through formal agreements. Also remember that you will need to demonstrate your loyalty to a Coconut group before you can penetrate its shell, and this process takes time. But once you make it inside, you will be entrusted with hard-won loyalty that is precious and productive. Go slowly to go quickly, but expect long-term relationships once you have passed the loyalty tests.

If you are a Coconut working with Peaches, focus on following the rules in order to be productive. Work relationships in Peach cultures might be fleeting, but the rules that define those relationships and work processes are often clearly spelled out and not very flexible. Follow social protocol specifically. Don't expect anything more than superficial hospitality initially. Avoid "pit-of-the-Peach" topics like sex, politics, or religion.

Both Peaches and Coconuts can ask these nonthreatening questions as they work with the opposite culture type:

- How can we build a working relationship together?
- What do I need to know about your culture to be successful?
- What do you want out of our business relationship?
- How can we make sure that your superior sees you as building a productive relationship with us?
- What differences do you see between the way we work and the way you work?

A Few Examples of Individualist and Collectivist Societies

The US and Australia are often rated as the most individualistic cultures in the world. In the US, there is constant political debate over what obligation, if any, the government has to less-productive individuals.

Collectivist societies, such as Japan and Korea, are fertile places to grow business because of these cultures' need to build groups. A social network created in a collectivist culture provides lifelong loyalty. If a product does not meet expectations, a refund is hardly sufficient for a Coconut. He or she would expect an apology because when a product is bought because of loyalty to another, the failure of that product is a violation of trust.

CHAPTER 5
How Do We Find What Is True?

Universalism   **TRUING**   Particularism

Question 2: How do we find what is true?

- What is the role of rules in society, and how important are they?
- How much flexibility is granted in following rules?
- What is the role of relationships in society?
- Who decides what it means to "do the right thing?"

A supplier had a breakdown in its manufacturing process that led to a violation of local environmental-protection laws. After careful study by the plant manager and a group of scientists and engineers, the problem was corrected. It was also determined that while there had been a violation of regulations, no actual harm had been done to the environment.

The study identified the cause of the problem as a shift manager who had failed to follow standard procedure. Several of the engineers on the study team wanted the shift manager to be fired and the plant manager to report the violation to the local authorities, even though no actual harm had taken place. The plant manager, on the other hand, wanted to deal with the shift manager privately and suggested that the shift manager would "learn from his mistake." The plant manager also resisted reporting the violation, saying, "No harm, no foul."

Both sides believed that they were taking the more ethical path. The engineers thought it was their obligation to "tell the truth at all costs, even if it hurts in the short term." The plant manager said, "It is my job to protect the people we have in this work community."

In this story, the engineers were Peaches and the plant manager was a Coconut. The conflict between them arose from a set of opposing cultural values: universalism (Peach) and particularism (Coconut).

The Universalist Peach and the Particularist Coconut

Universalism is a deep drive to establish and follow rules consistently. It is part of the way that a Peach society keeps a level playing field and holds people accountable. In a Peach culture, if a relationship comes into conflict with rules, the rules will win out. To this point, we have discussed a few ideas that form the pit in the Peach metaphor. The fact that there is a limit to what one will do for a friend, and that certain topics are off limits in the workplace are examples. The Universalist ideal of a set of rules that apply equally to everyone is also a driving force that creates the boundaries of the pit.

Particularism is not really concerned with following rules consistently. Rules are used in particularist cultures, but not the same way as they are used in universalist cultures. In particularism, relationships are paramount. Adherence to rules can be dealt with on a case-by-case basis. In a Coconut culture, if rules come into conflict with a relationship, the relationship will win out.

It is easy for Peaches and Coconuts to each feel that the other culture type is wrong in this aspect and to criticize the outcomes. But both the Peach way and the Coconut way can lead to good outcomes and build long-term value. Be patient and try to understand the other culture type's point of view as you read this chapter.

Using Universalism and Particularism to Find Truth

One process through which cultures build a foundation for truth is with stories or myths. Myths are the narrative stories of culture. We have come to see them as ancient, but they can be modern too. Cultures around the world have myths about the past, religious beliefs, sports heroes, political leaders, inventors, business builders, and other topics. At the core of a culture's myths are the values that that culture venerates. Bravery, freedom, innovation, loyalty, and creation are some of the values emphasized in myths.

For example, a Chinese creation myth describes the beginning as only chaos. Chaos eventually formed into a cosmic egg. As the perfectly opposite forces of yin and yang became balanced, Pangu—a hairy, fur-clad giant with horns—emerged from the egg and began the task of creating the world. Pangu separated yin (representing the earth) from yang (representing the sky). This task took eighteen thousand years. When it was complete, Pangu died. Its breath became the wind, its blood formed the rivers, its muscles became the fertile land, and its bone marrow became diamonds. This myth highlights the values of creation, order, and balance.

While most Chinese schoolchildren learn the creation myths of their culture, few believe them. Creation myths have been replaced in modern times by more-scientific and more-rational ways of telling how humans, the world, and the universe were formed. While myths are often relegated to academic study, Joseph Campbell taught that they also function in our everyday lives to tell us what is right, what is wrong, and what is true.[4] Thus, aside from their metaphysical and cosmological functions, myths also have a sociological function. A myth can confirm a social order, including the values and ideals that form core cultural beliefs. A myth also provides psychological relief as it connects people with their genealogies, families, communities, and ideals.

Some people see the myths they grew up with as useful stories that project common values. Others see myths as a record of literal events. In Western culture, the gulf between creationists and evolutionists, for example, is evidence not only of competing myths but also of disagreement about what in myths is literal.

It may be tempting to use myths to determine cultural values, but this technique is difficult because we do not always know how literal or how common a given myth might be. But myths do help us see how truing—the process of making something true—occurs in a culture. To understand truing in a given culture, we must ask questions like these:

- How much weight does the culture give to logic, reliability, standardization, and replication when a statement is made?
- How do we know that a statement is true?
- Why do we know that a statement is true?

There are two main types of truing; one corresponds to Peach cultures and the other corresponds to Coconut cultures. Peach cultures provide universal laws that tell people what is true. Coconut cultures believe that truth is not as important as maintaining a relationship with someone in a social network. Another way of saying this is that for Peaches, truth is in the universe. Humans can *identify* truth, but the laws that *define* it are established by God, gods, or science. For Coconuts, truth is in relationships. A Coconut might explain this concept by saying, "I cannot know the universe, but I can know my neighbor, my father or mother, or my president or elder. They tell me what is true. Because I have a relationship with them that is sure, I follow."

Universalist Peaches

Most universalist cultures are Peach and are based on the assumption that there is a universal law that prescribes the one right way of doing things. This law applies to everyone equally. Universal human-rights declarations, the Ten Commandments, and "the enlightened way" are all examples of universal laws.

Universalist cultures often grow out of highly religious societies in which universal law comes from one or more deities. For example, many Christians believe that God gave laws to humans through Jesus Christ and other messengers. A person who does not follow God's laws is punished in the afterlife, but a person who follows God's laws is rewarded with a place in heaven. What exactly are God's laws? That is open to interpretation, but many Christians believe that acts such as stealing, murder, lying, and adultery are wrong because they are contrary to God's laws.

While most Western cultures advocate the separation of church and state, the "laws of the land" (codes that all people must follow regardless of their religious beliefs) are generally based on what were once Christian or other religious ideals. Core Western legal documents such as the Magna Carta, the Declaration of Independence, and the Constitution of the United States all invoke or allude to God in their statements regarding property ownership, the sanctity of life, and the definition of morality. As beliefs change, legal interpretations also change, creating controversy. But core values, such as telling the truth or being faithful in relationships, do not change much over time, even if a society seems less committed to their practice.

It is not just Christians who are universalists. Muslims, for instance, can also be seen as universalists. The word *Islam* means "submission to Allah" (the name used for God in Arabic, the original language of the Koran). Those who submit to Allah are following Allah's will. Muslims believe that Allah sent the holy Koran and the prophet Muhammad to establish universal peace and harmony. Every year, close to three million devout Muslims from all over the world complete the hajj, a once-in-a-lifetime pilgrimage to Mecca that is required of all financially and physically able Muslims. In that setting, no one person stands out, because everyone dresses in similar clothing as part of the worship ceremonies.

It would be a mistake to assume that universalism is only religiously based. Many people are not religious in their personal practices yet are highly universalist. For example, some people who believe in scientific law and rationality are universalists. They believe that scientific principles and patterns govern the universe and that the closer humans operate to those principles and patterns, the better the outcome will be. Thomas Kuhn[5] pointed out that science is done in communities and that when one scientist challenges long-held standards, he or she displaces another scientist. Social conflict and controversy ensue, but in this evolution of scientific knowledge, it is assumed that humans and their understanding are evolving and getting closer to the universal laws of the universe (hence the name). Thus, the engineers in the story that opened this chapter are universalists in more than one way.

A familiar extension of universalism is social science, which is highly prescriptive. The discipline of psychology focuses on naming deviances from "normal" thinking and behavior. Sociology prescribes and describes appropriate family structures and organizational behavior along with ideal organizational forms. Even Western art prescribes a certain aesthetic. All these fields of study have roots in a universalist perspective.

The mostly widely accepted form of universalism today is the rule of law, in which certain standards apply equally to everyone and police and justice systems are in place to enforce social contracts. This type of universalism also affects how Peaches do business. In Peach cultures, business contracts determine each party's responsibilities, and fair penalties enforce the will of the contract. Standard practices govern accounting and other business functions. Because relationships are not the highest priority, Peaches prefer to minimize socializing and immediately begin working on business tasks.

Particularist Coconuts

In contrast, for the plant manager described at the beginning of this chapter, work is life. His first loyalty is not to laws, numbers, measurements, or regulations. His first loyalty is to those who give their time every day to build the community of the plant. His employees see him as a father figure or patriarch. They come to him for personal advice and protection.

People who practice extensive social networking and follow strong local rules for that networking are called particularists. They believe that their relationships are more important than universal truth. Particularism arises in societies where central authority is abusive or does not exist. In Western culture, the lawless "wild, wild West" was particularist. If the sheriff knew and trusted you, you were treated with privilege and respect. If he did not know you, or if there was no sheriff, you had to live by a different set of rules. Similarly, China—ruled either by an emperor or by a dictator for most of its history—has emerged as a particularist society. Its concept of *guanxi* includes the idea of having a trusted social network.

Particularism affects how Coconuts do business. Since relationships are the highest priority, Coconuts prefer to socialize and get to know others before beginning business tasks. Agreements tend to be flexible and may not be formalized in contracts.

Mixing Universalism and Particularism

In some cultures, there are strong strains of both universalism and particularism. For instance, some researchers have measured universalism and particularism by region in the US. Overall, the US is a universalist country. The rule of law means that all individuals must fulfill certain responsibilities. Everyone must pay taxes, though the amounts differ with one's income level. The speed limit is the same for everyone. Still, research suggests that some regions in the US are more particularist than others. Regions in the southern, central, and western parts of the country—where the rate of church attendance is higher—tend to be more particularist. Even though these groups are part of a larger Peach culture, the strong feelings and shared values that differ from the larger culture create something of a shell around the group. Therefore, they may exhibit characteristics of both Peach and Coconut cutlures.

Case Study: The Ute Indian Reservation

Regardless of whether a given society is universalist or particularist, eventually someone violates the rules. When that happens, does the greater punishment come from a Coconut culture or a Peach culture? The Uintah and Ouray Indian Reservation or Ute Indian Reservation in the US state of Utah, where we have done much work, provides a useful case study.

The reservation is a checkerboard of tribal and public lands. Determining the jurisdiction of the various local and federal police forces is problematic. On one block, a Ute Tribe member who is arrested for reckless driving might be under the jurisdiction of the non-tribal county sheriff, while on another block he or she might be subject to the tribal police force run by the Bureau of Indian Affairs (BIA), a federal agency.

The sheriff complains that when the BIA officers arrest a Tribe member for a minor violation, "they just seem to let them off." The truth is that the BIA officers are part of a Coconut culture, and their actions reflect Coconut values. To Coconuts, rules are subordinate to the relationships that a person has with family and Tribal members. The BIA officers will often take an offender directly to a Tribal elder (the closest relative who knows and can speak with the person) without the booking, holding, and court-hearing procedures that are expected in a universalist culture. The elder can then talk with the violator and describe how the violator has damaged relationships. As one elder explained, he says to offenders, "You have shamed me, your parents, your family, and your people by committing this act. What can you do now to make it right?"

The sheriff, on the other hand, comes from a Peach culture and follows universalist principles in how he treats offenders. If a person is arrested, police process is followed specifically, including handcuffs, jail cells, bail hearings, preliminary hearings, etc., under the principle that "all people are equal before the law."

Self-Assessment: Universalist or Particularist?

By now, you may be getting a sense of whether you are a universalist or a particularist. To determine your category more specifically, fill out the table below by circling the option from each pair that best describes your preference *most of the time.* (Note that the choices may be more difficult than those from the self-assessment in chapter 4. People's preferences are often not as strong in this dimension of culture.) The results are nonscientific, but they are sufficient to trigger the self-examination required to establish Culture3 Dialogue.

Universalism   **TRUING**   Particularism

I prefer:	
When rules are rules	When rules are modified based on trust
To trust a contract	To trust a relationship
Objective measurements	Relative measurements
That my work stays at work	That my work is part of my personal life
To trust numbers	To trust people
To protect a process	To protect people
That contracts define relationships	That relationships define contracts
To get down to business	To get to know people
Maintaining and assessing quality	Having the right people in the right places
One right way	Many right ways

If you circled more answers in the left column, you are likely a Peach (universalist). If you circled more answers in the right column, you are likely a Coconut (particularist).

Peach cultures tend to be universalist. The cultures of the US, Australia, the UK, Germany, Austria, Scandinavian countries, and Singapore fall into this category. Coconut cultures tend to be particularist. This category includes the cultures of Indonesia, South Korea, Japan, and Latin American countries.

Armed with this understanding of how you determine what is true, let's examine some common difficulties (and solutions to them) that arise when working with people who determine truth in other ways.

Establishing Culture3 Dialogue

Universalism and particularism guide behavior more than any other aspect of culture does, but they are also culture's least-visible aspect. We often think that "our" way is the right way of doing things. Thus, conflict between universalists and particularists is often deep and based on what each side believes to be moral judgments.

If you are a Coconut working with Peaches, don't be offended by their "get-down-to-business" attitude. This does not mean that your Peach colleagues do not care about you or your team; it means that they are following their higher priority of the big picture of the business. Also, be prepared with rational arguments and formal presentations. Peaches like data and objective measures. These details help them feel justified in taking action. If there is a change required, remember that contracts and rules can be modified, but generally those modifications need to come in writing. In negotiations, Peaches will push to get a compromise and close the deal. A compromise does not represent a loss of face to a Peach; it is part of the job.

If you are a Peach, be patient while ceremony and socialization are used to build relationships and trust with a Coconut. Expect individual attention and special favors, including gifts, directed towards you. These are not bribes but ways of offering trust and friendship. Agreements will come only after relationships are established. It is assumed that relationships will be mutually beneficial and could be modified when they aren't. Consider building in contingencies that do not appear to lock in an agreement. Your Coconut host will be more comfortable when there is flexibility.

Chapter 6
How Do We Work Together as a Team?

Low Power Distance   **TEAM**   High Power Distance

Question 3: How do we work together as a team?

- How is team membership determined?
- How equal are team members?
- How are conflicts resolved?
- How are work processes determined?

Imagine yourself flying into Tahiti to set up a branch office. You're from the US and used to working in London, New York City, and the midwestern US, where associates greet each other with a handshake. You're wearing a business suit because you expect to be greeted by your host. When you arrive in Tahiti, to your surprise, your host places a lei over your head and gives you a kiss on each cheek (known as a *bise*). He then introduces you to his family members, who in turn each give you a *bise*. You have just left a moderate-power-distance culture and entered a very-low-power-distance culture.

Power distance is the extent to which the less-powerful members of organizations or groups expect and accept that power is distributed unequally. In Tahiti, while you may consider yourself an important businessperson, you are not seen as any more important than the person greeting you. Your status comes not from the fact that you are in control of a business deal but rather from the fact that you are a guest in Tahiti.

Contrast Tahiti with China and its strict hierarchies (both imperial and Communist). Generally, Chinese people assume a large distance between people of authority and people who do not have authority. For instance, a US contractor was hosted by an important Chinese business executive, who sent his driver to pick the contractor up at the hotel and drive him to the meeting location. Drivers in China, like butlers in the UK, are to be seen and not heard; they help but don't get in the way. In addition, a common Chinese saying states, "The professor is always right." This status is often transferred to guests and foreign visitors. The contractor was introduced to the driver as a professor, but he might as well have been introduced as a military general. This driver was used to carrying important people and treated the contractor with great respect and professionalism.

These factors later led to a perplexing situation for the contractor. On the return trip to the hotel, the car entered a roundabout. Confused, the driver went around several times as he tried to figure out which exit would lead him to the hotel. Seeing the driver's confusion, the contractor suggested an exit that looked familiar, but by then the driver was already committed to taking another exit, which turned out to be the correct route. But the driver entered the parking lot of the hotel, turned around without stopping, and went back to the roundabout and took the exit that the contractor had recommended. In broken English, the driver said, "The professor is always right."

Both of these stories demonstrate the two ways in which teams can work together: low power distance (Peach) or high power distance (Coconut). This dimension of culture can cause significant discomfort and frustration when opposite culture types interact. However, as with all dimensions of culture, these gaps can be bridged.

The Low-Power-Distance Peach and the High-Power-Distance Coconut

It is easy to get through the skin of a ripe peach with a dull knife, but the same knife will never penetrate (or even dent) the outer shell of a coconut. This imagery gives important insights into the difference between Peach (low-power-distance) and Coconut (high-power-distance) cultures.

Peach cultures are typically more egalitarian or low power distance. Many leaders will try to minimize their power or authority in casual or social situations. Even governors of US States will blend in with the groups they travel with on trade missions. This can be frustrating for leaders in Coconut cultures who are trying to determine who the leaders are. In these low-power distance societies, it is your performance and obedience to rules that determines your proximity to power.

Coconut cultures, on the other hand, typically have very clear hierarchies or high power distance. There are many social norms and even specific language to reinforce and make it clear who is higher and who is lower in status. In these societies, your relationships and your social position determine your proximity to power. In this system it is who you know, not what you know, matters most.

Power distance also shows in the way people use personal space. In high-power-distance cultures, a handshake is often the limit of the physical contact between business people. But in low-power-distance cultures, hugs, embraces, and even kisses are often offered freely, even to strangers.

Peach Case Study: The US

The Peach-oriented United States was founded on the premise of equality for all, and this value manifests itself in the famously low-power-distance US culture. In the 1930s, renowned violinist Roman Totenberg played for royalty in England. After the performance and the applause, he was required to leave the stage by walking backwards so as to not turn his back on the queen. A few weeks later, Totenberg performed for US President Franklin Roosevelt at the White House. After the performance, Totenberg was invited into the president's living quarters, and he sat on chairs with the president and the First Lady and had tea. After that close encounter, Totenberg made plans to immigrate to the US.

As Totenberg's visit with President Roosevelt demonstrates, even those who aspire to high positions in US politics are expected to maintain low power distance. During US presidential campaigns, candidates are expected to go city-to-city and town-to-town shaking hands, kissing babies, and meeting as many people as possible. A few years ago, newspapers included an article about presidential candidates and compared how much each of the candidates tipped hotel maids. Their treatment of hotel maids was seen as a way of measuring their respect for people of the working class. This ability to wield considerable authority while seeming "just like the rest of us" is considered a valued characteristic in a leader.

People from the US also seem to want low power distance, or the air of the "common man," in their heroes, including movie stars, professional athletes, and celebrities. A "good" movie star, athlete, or celebrity is one who will meet with the people, visit hospitals, and perform community service. Famous people who do not participate in such activities may be labeled "snobs" or said to "think they're better than us."

CocoPeach with High Power Distance Case Study: The UK

Some democratic societies, like the UK, have largely Peach cultures but also have clearly prescribed social hierarchies that preserve distance between those who have higher social status and those who do not. In these societies, people of one class live near each other and do not mingle unnecessarily with people of another class. The notion of public schools is all right, as long as one's children can go to school with children of their class and not with children of another class. In these high-power-distance cultures, it is often assumed that the upper class receives the privileges and tries to preserve the hierarchy. But the lower classes are often equally protective of the hierarchy because in a high-power-distance society, even the lower classes value their places of belonging.

Coconut Case Study: China

An even higher power distance is expected in Coconut China. Subordinates acknowledge the power of superiors, and people expect to be defined by their formal hierarchical positions. In particular, titles carry a great deal of weight and define the status of the people who hold them. It is important for a person of status to meet only with someone of similar status. While *manager* is a title of high esteem in China, a *director* is even more important. Thus, directors meet with directors but not with managers, vice presidents meet with vice presidents but not with presidents, etc. It is not uncommon for high-titled Western business leaders to accompany lower-ranking employees to China just so that their teams can have access to the high-titled Chinese leaders who make business decisions.

In the high-power-distance culture of China, it does not matter *what* is actually correct; it only matters *who* is acknowledged as being correct. Therefore, establishing agreement with or outranking the right people in the right places is critical to getting things done.

Case Study: Extreme Power Distances

The highest-power-distance cultures sequester high-status individuals away from low-status individuals. In these societies, the high-status people only emerge in ceremony. One example is the culture of imperial China during the period when the emperors lived in the Forbidden City, which only they, their families, and their servants could enter. The emperors would leave the gilded prison only to hold court with the nobility.

On the other hand, some cultures have extremely low power distance. One example is a US-based global company that we have visited many times: Amway Corporation. The surviving founder and his family, who are also owners are accessible to all employees. The company's annual Christmas party is held in an arena with over ten thousand seats, where ninety-three-year-old cofounder Rich DeVoss reads the Christmas story. "I feel like he is my dad telling me a story," said one employee. "Later he gave me a hug, and I had never even met him. He asked what I did and thanked me for my service."

Case Study: Power Distances in Conflict

Gary Locke, a former US ambassador to China, caused a controversy before he even arrived at his first meeting. On his first trip to China, Locke took his backpack for carry-on luggage and bought a Starbucks coffee while waiting to board his flight. In the line at Starbucks, a Chinese national recognized the new ambassador and took a cell-phone photo, which he quickly texted to China.

In the high-power-distance culture of China, an ambassador would not be seen standing in line, wearing a backpack, or picking up his or her own food. The Chinese media labeled this "peasant" behavior. But the flames were fanned even more when it was discovered that Locke had flown coach fare, "'like some kind of poverty-stricken farmer's cattle.'"[6]

Self-Assessment: Low Power Distance or High Power Distance?

By now, you may be getting a sense of whether you prefer low power distance or high power distance. To determine your category more specifically, fill out the table below by circling the option from each pair that best describes your preference *most of the time*. The results are non-scientific, but they are sufficient to trigger the self-examination required to establish Culture3 Dialogue.

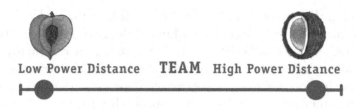

Low Power Distance   **TEAM**   High Power Distance

I prefer:	
To greet leaders the same way as I greet peers	To formally greet leaders
Status determined by contribution	Status determined by title
Flat organizations	Layered organizations
Shared leadership	Defined leadership roles
Being consulted about a decision	Being told what to do
Collaborative teamwork	Formal rules and procedures
Hugs and kisses	Handshakes and bowing
Equal privileges for all	Special privileges for leaders
A colleague as a boss	A parental figure as a boss
All types of jobs have equal status	White collar over blue collar

If you circled more answers in the left column, you are likely a Peach (prefer low power distance). If you circled more answers in the right column, you are likely a Coconut (prefer high power distance).

Now that you know the amount of power distance you prefer, let's examine how to effectively work with people who prefer different amounts.

Establishing Culture3 Dialogue

Power distance is one of the most-obvious and least-subtle cultural dimensions. On a first encounter, you can tell whether members of a particular culture greet others with a hug, a handshake, or something else. You may feel awkward demonstrating more or less power distance than you are used to, but you can build trust by learning and participating in greetings from your colleagues' cultures. In Japanese culture, for instance, the presentation of the business card is taken to a ritualistic level. The card itself is important not only for the information that it contains but also for the fact that it was gifted to you as a representation of status. In Japan, a person holds his or her card with both hands and bows while presenting that card to you. You bow as you receive the card with both hands, thanking the person and looking at the card. Additional bows and expressions of thanks will follow. This ceremony may seem over the top if you are a Peach and used to simply handing someone your business card. But in Coconut, high-power-distance Japanese society, it is crucial to demonstrate respect for a person's status in this way.

Beyond greetings, it is important to learn the other rituals of formal power in the cultures of your colleagues. Often these rituals are reserved for public contexts. If you are invited into a private setting, more-informal and less-ritualistic behavior is allowed. But it is extremely important to wait to be invited into the private space.

For example, in the US, formal business gatherings like board meetings or leadership retreats are structured and have fairly high power distance. In such events, high-status people control the process and invite others to contribute to the content of the meetings. While all attendees might be "casual Friday" in their dress, seating assignments are carefully charted, and deference is given to the opinion leaders. But later in that same gathering, a social event, trip to a bar, or golf game might be scheduled. In this context, power distance is low. People are more equal, and everyone is free to comment on both the content and the process of the meetings.

If you are from a low-power-distance culture, it can be easy to fall into the trap of believing that high power distance is created by high-status people to preserve their privileges. However, this idea is not completely accurate. Low-status members of such cultures often support the high level of power distance in hopes of someday moving up the hierarchy. Meanwhile, they enjoy the security of having a parental figure at the head of the organizational family.

CHAPTER 7
How Do We Deal with Time?

Monochronic   **TIME**   Polychronic

Question 4: How do we deal with time?

- Is time linear or cyclical?
- How past-/present-/future-oriented are we?
- How do we conduct meetings?
- What do we consider to be a deadline?
- How do we hold each other accountable for meeting deadlines?

Imagine that you are a businessperson and have been invited to a meeting with an important global-business partner. The appointment is set for ten o'clock in the morning, and you dutifully arrive five minutes early. An administrative assistant seats you on a couch outside an office, where you wait for fifteen or twenty minutes. As you grow increasingly impatient, you try to focus on how you hope this meeting will proceed. You have a carefully planned agenda. Each slide of your presentation deck carefully builds upon the previous point, offering evidence and laying out an argument that leads to your set of recommendations. You are proud of the way you have followed all the rules laid out (formally or informally) in the ceremony known as "the business presentation."

After waiting about thirty minutes, you are invited into the office. You're introduced to five different people. Nothing about the seating or arrangement indicates who the decision maker is. It is only through introductions that this is made clear. Instead of placing you at the front of the room, your host sits you with his colleagues around a table, and you are invited to join them for a conversation. Instead of getting down to business, they engage in small talk about families, politics, travel, and the weather.

When you finally begin your presentation, you are bombarded with questions. You suggest politely that the group listen to your presentation before they ask questions. But the group has a different sense of process. They want to engage you immediately in questions without taking time to fully understand your proposal.

Would you be frustrated? Would this be a difficult situation for you to manage?

According to anthropologist Edward T. Hall, how time is viewed is a common cultural friction point. In his 1959 book *The Silent Language*,[7] Hall introduced the terms *monochronic* and *polychronic* to describe how cultures view time.

Similarly, a culture may look at time with a short-term orientation or a long-term orientation. Cultures with thousands of years of written or oral history, like China and some parts of Europe, tend to look at time differently than cultures that are doing everything for the first time (relatively speaking), such as the US.

These two binaries—monochronic versus polychronic and short-term orientation versus long-term orientation—help explain the frustrations between the presenter and the hosts in the story.

Monochronic Peaches

Peach cultures are monochronic. Their members see time as linear and incremental, a single line that extends to infinity without beginning or end. People are expected to do one thing at a time, and there are rules for managing time. Peaches won't tolerate lateness or interruptions. These views suggest that it is appropriate to track time by the quarter, month, week, day, hour, minute, or second. Time is valued and counted just as money is valued and counted. Meetings start on time and are controlled by an agenda. There is a bias towards rational presentations. And there is little or no small talk.

Monochronic cultures also tend to be short-term oriented. They focus on immediacy. In the US, for instance, savings rates are fairly low and impulse actions, like a wild spring break or a trip to Las Vegas, are valued. Quarterly results that put a company ahead of the competition are more important than sustainable results over time. Relationships are utilitarian and useful only if they help meet immediate goals. "Pioneers," "firsts," and "new" are all touted and valued. Little time is spent reflecting on the past or on writing history.

Short-term-oriented cultures tend to be less connected to ancestors, tradition, and ceremony. (Those with a long-term orientation see this behavior as selfish and self-indulgent.) The ideas of "carpe diem," "being in the present," and "here today, gone tomorrow" suggest that now is more important than later. Traditions not supported by this belief are discarded. For example, fifty years ago it was considered shameful for a man and a woman to live together without being married. Today, that lifestyle choice is considered normal in the US and most of Europe.

Clearly, the presenter in the story above is a Peach. This person expects to make a linear (i.e., interruption-free), logical, rational presentation to form the basis of a decision. His or her monochronic bias is to present a logical case for a predetermined plan of action. This is not a time to start from scratch, to get input or to discuss possible plans. It's a time for the individual, assigned to come up with a plan, to present his or her case. This approach assumes that human beings are rational and that the best decisions are supported with accepted evidence.

Polychronic Coconuts

Coconut cultures are polychronic. They typically have long histories, and thus Coconuts assume that no problem is new; today's difficulties are simply variations on problems that existed a hundred years ago, and they will return later in a different form. The rules that guide a Peach, such as presentation protocols and tracking time spent, are less important to a Coconut than relationships. There is no prescribed way of solving problems. Problems are opportunities to relate to each other, and in some cases, problems are created in order to cause an interaction.

Polychronic cultures see time as complex, seasonal, and cyclical. In such cultures, it is not important to be on time for, say, a wedding, but the wedding itself is very important. The typical communication mode in a polychronic culture is discussion and dialogue because the focus is on the relationships and achieving consensus with the group. It is acceptable to interrupt someone and ask questions because it is in the interaction that relationships are built. Furthermore, it is assumed that each person in the room—whether or not he or she is an expert—might understand some important aspect of the decision to be made. Thus, it is important to seek consensus because the wisdom of the group is greater than that of any individual. And since everyone is to have a relationship with everyone else, all are invited to participate in the conversation.

Polychronic cultures also tend to be long-term oriented. They stress pragmatism, thrift, and perseverance. It is assumed that ancestors have traveled the current path before and that coming generations will travel it again. In long-term-oriented societies, there is a deep respect for tradition, genealogy, and elders. Often the giving of gifts and favors is seen as the best way to show that respect. Some long-term-oriented cultures even practice ancestor worship.

Long-term-oriented cultures tend to feel great responsibility for the next generation. In Japan, for instance, the savings rate for the average family is quite high. Members of these cultures push or even shame their children into performing at a higher level than the previous generation. They look back on previous generations and maintain traditions even when current beliefs do not support those traditions. For example, few (if any) people in China today believe in dragons, but every restaurant has a pair of dragon statues by the entrance for good luck. In Japan, few people believe in Shinto spirits, but many couples are married in Shinto ceremonies.

The members of the host group in the story above are clearly Coconuts. Starting a meeting on time is less important to them than strengthening their relationships with each other and with the presenter. They also want to engage the presenter in dialogue instead of simply hearing the presentation.

It's easy to see how a monochronic person might be troubled by a polychronic cultural environment and vice versa. Let's look at some specific examples of monochronic and polychronic cultures for more insight on how to navigate this potential source of frustration.

Peach Case Study: The US

Most Western business practices and norms, manufacturing process, and even computer programs assume, impose, and follow monochronic values. In particular, US culture is highly monochronic. This society provides a useful case study of how monochronic cultures function.

People from the US teach children to be on time from an early age. As children grow older, they are pushed to meet deadlines and maximize efficiency. For people from the US, even leisure time is identified and labeled a "break," a "vacation," a "holiday," or a "retirement."

This view of time appears in reading material too. Any US bookstore has many items in the self-help and business sections on how to manage time. These books teach that productivity lies in following the rules: be on time, keep meetings short and to the point, and make presentations that are rational, logical, and persuasive. The wildly popular book *The Seven Habits of Highly Effective People*, written by Stephen R. Covey,[8] focuses on the increased efficiencies gained by adapting monochronic values that "begin with the end in mind." It is assumed by Covey and many other self-help authors that even young schoolchildren can benefit from having an explicit agenda for the day with a highly structured and clearly articulated set of goals and values. This approach is assumed to be the norm and the "right" way to do things.

Case Study: Switching between Polychronic and Monochronic Cultures

It can be confusing to switch from working in a monochronic culture to working in a polychronic one or vice versa. The experiences of Marion, an employee at a large pharmaceutical company, provide some useful insights for anyone who must shift in this way.

Marion was assigned to lead the rollout of an internal retirement program into European countries. On the first day of her trip, she was scheduled to give a presentation to a group of senior-level managers in France. She arrived at Charles de Gaulle Airport from London at about nine o'clock in the morning. However, between her driver's late arrival at the airport and the absence of a sign identifying him as Marion's driver, they were thirty minutes late leaving the airport. The driver was casual and made conversation as he drove Marion to the company campus in central Paris. He said he was an intern working at the company.

When Marion arrived at the campus, an administrative staff member met her at the door, took her to a conference room, and helped her set up her media for the presentation. The meeting was scheduled to begin at ten o'clock, but the first participant didn't wander in until 10:30. By 10:45, the entire group had arrived, but they were talking with each other about the business of the day, paying little attention to Marion except to greet and welcome her. By about eleven o'clock, the group's senior member suggested that they get down to business. For about forty-five minutes, everyone focused intensely on Marion's presentation, moving through it quickly and peppering her with questions.

Just as Marian thought she was gaining momentum, at 11:45, the senior member suggested that the group pause for a moment and discuss where they would be dining for lunch. A wild conversation ensued, including a passionate argument about the best restaurant within driving distance of the campus. It took thirty minutes for the group to agree on a restaurant. Reservations were quickly made, and everyone headed to the restaurant amid much conversation about Marion's presentation. Over lunch, the group continued to ask Marion lots of questions about her presentation. The lunch finished at about 2:15, and by 2:45 the group was back in the conference room listening to Marion finish her presentation, which she completed by four o'clock.

The next day, Marion flew to Frankfurt, Germany, where she was to make the same presentation. She arrived at about nine o'clock in the morning to find a driver waiting, holding a sign with her name on it. The driver did not speak to Marion except to acknowledge instructions. He seated her in the back of a limousine and drove her directly to the company campus.

Marion's meeting was scheduled to start at ten o'clock. Participants began arriving at 9:50. They each greeted her with a handshake and then quickly sat down. At ten o'clock, Marion began her presentation. There was little discussion and no questions.

After two hours, the senior member of the group excused the team for a one-hour lunch break. Everyone left the room, and Marion wondered where she would get her lunch. Eventually she was able to get a sandwich from the internal snack bar. At one o'clock, the group returned, and by 1:05, Marion was continuing her presentation. After a precisely scheduled tea break at 3 p.m., Marion finished her presentation at four o'clock.

Marion's report about these two presentations noted that both groups had heard the information, understood, and asked questions. But the groups had completely different styles for learning and processing that information.

The French group was clearly polychronic. While it seemed as though having lunch was the most important event of the day, these CocoPeaches (see the country report on France) knew the importance of building a good, trusting relationship with a presenter. They believed that this goal was best accomplished in a social environment where ideas could be tested and behaviors observed.

In contrast, the German team was clearly monochronic. As Peaches, they wanted a linear, rational, and logical presentation. They relied on Marion to provide information before they would process and ask questions.

Potential Time-View Conflicts

The contrast between monochronic and polychronic styles and between short- and long-term orientations can be an especially problematic issue on multicultural work teams. In particular, Peaches often have trouble seeing the value of Coconut perspectives on time. A polychronic, long-term-oriented style can create an environment in which creativity flows, complexity is knowledge, and new ideas can be created through the impromptu interactions that naturally occur. But a Peach may ask, "Why are we wasting time? How will I get anything done in all this chaos? How is this going to help us meet our quarterly goals?"

Interestingly, though, while most technological innovations for business (such as email and PowerPoint) support monochronic work processes, many tech companies deliberately create polychronic work environments to spur creativity. They want both the measurable productivity that comes from monochronic style and the creative advantages that come from polychronic style. Similarly, an astute and effective businessperson needs to be able to work in and adapt to both kinds of cultures.

Self-Assessment: Monochronic or Polychronic, Short-Term or Long-Term Orientation?

By now, you may be getting a sense of whether you are monochronic or polychronic and whether you are short-term oriented or long-term oriented. To determine your category more specifically, fill out the table below by circling the option from each pair that best describes your preference *most of the time*. The results are nonscientific, but they are sufficient to trigger the self-examination required to establish Culture3 Dialogue.

Particularly for this self-assessment, remember that while we all have tendencies, our own preferences vary among circumstances and depend on our roles. A reporter named Jacqueline, for example, was always bucking deadlines at her newspaper, pushing the schedule right to the limit. But when she was made editor, she became extremely demanding of the other reporters regarding deadlines. When asked about this, Jacqueline said, "When I was a reporter, my role was to fight for the story. As an editor, my role is to fight for the newspaper."

Monochronic   TIME   Polychronic

I prefer:	
Meetings with agendas	Meetings that are free-flowing
Coming to work at the same time every day	A flexible work schedule
Deadlines that are set	Deadlines that allow for flexibility
Specific expectations	Specific outcomes
Measuring my progress towards a goal	Measuring who likes my work
Having a common process for everything	Trying different ways
Having quarterly performance assessments	Having annual performance assessments
Assessment based on progress	Assessment based on innovation
To take things one step at a time	To see the whole first
To focus on my job	To focus on the company

If you circled more answers in the left column, you are likely a Peach (monochronic and short-term oriented). If you circled more answers in the right column, you are likely a Coconut (polychronic and long-term oriented). Very few people prefer just one side in all circumstances.

With this understanding of how you view time, let's examine how to effectively work with people who have different conceptions of time.

Establishing Culture3 Dialogue

As a leader, you can see many places where values and behaviors related to time affect the way your team works. In this section, we will deal with three of the most obvious issues that can arise.

Deadlines

If you are a Peach, you are likely to see a deadline as something that is fixed, important, and immovable. Your Coconut counterparts, however, are more likely to see the deadline as a guideline. Especially if they have a good relationship with you or with other team members, they will assume that you understand the complexities and changing issues that may affect when they can actually finish the work.

If you are a Coconut and have Peaches on your team, they are likely to want more structure and firm commitments than you are giving. They will want to see incremental progress toward goals and to have incremental feedback on that progress. If they do not have that kind of structure and feedback, they will likely feel that the team is drifting without leadership.

Measuring Progress and Providing Guidelines

If you are a Peach, you are likely to measure progress by how much time is being committed to a task. Coconut colleagues are likely to measure progress by quality of results rather than by time spent on the task. Peach team members want to agree on work conditions and have well-defined time frames and processes. Coconut team members have many ways to get to the same place. They want more autonomy, less definition about time and process, and more definition about relationships. They want more room for innovation and creative conversation.

We observed one team in which these competing priorities were balanced well. Some team members were from a Latino culture, and they felt that the team's project-management software, which identified deadlines and specific processes, was too confining. The team leader wisely stepped in. To counter the highly structured approach of the software, he carefully negotiated open-ended conference calls that allowed for free-flowing dialogue about work processes. The Coconut team members still said that the process was too structured, but they complied. The Peach team members said that the long conference calls were not always the best use of time, but they complied. The entire team, however, saw the project as a success.

Meeting Management

Peach team members need to know in advance what a meeting is for and why it is worth their time. Once in the meeting, they need a clear agenda to see that they are on task and making progress. Coconut team members need open dialogue and chances to build relationships. One Coconut team member said that the best things that happened at extended meetings were the breaks—not because he could catch up on phone calls or email, but because breaks were unstructured time where he could do important relationship building.

A team leader managing both Peaches and Coconuts should explain these principles to all and provide both structured and unstructured time in meetings. Without both, the team will miss out on valuable contributions from all team members.

Understanding Time on a Dark Night in Samoa

Because their conceptions of time are so different, Peaches and Coconuts can struggle to find enough common ground to work together. Coauthor Scott Hammond related his own experience in coming to an understanding of the opposite viewpoint:

> I was sent by my company to evaluate a program on a remote island in Samoa. After a short plane ride and a long, bumpy car ride to the only hotel on the island, I settled into the clean but simple room near the water's edge. The eight-room hotel was on the northern shore of the island, on a point surrounded by blue ocean on three sides. But the entire island did not have a single mile of paved roads, and the only taxi had taken ninety minutes to drive ten miles. I was tired and needed to connect with my office, so I was looking forward to getting to my room and getting to my email.
>
> Once in the room, I tried to connect, but there was no Wi-Fi signal. I returned to the front desk and launched into my complaint, but the clerk told me that there was no internet. I said, "It says in the brochure that this hotel has internet," but the clerk just said, "No internet." I don't think he knew the difference between *internet* and *fishing net*.
>
> When I returned to my room, I started drafting the emails that I hoped to send the next day from the company's local campus. My computer needed charging, but the power went out. It was completely dark. Once again I went to the desk, because the phone in my room also did not work. I was pissed off — mad. How could I get my work done in this kind of environment?

The desk clerk was nowhere to be found, so I wandered through the lobby and out onto the lanai [porch or veranda]. There was a group of men sitting in a half circle, facing the sea. I asked, "When will the power be on?"

Ignoring my question, one of men said in a quiet voice, "Sit down with us, brother." I sat, and as I did, another man began softly strumming his ukulele. Another began singing, and soon everyone had joined in. In the dark, a bowl of fruit was passed my way, followed by a cup filled with sweet liquid that I could not identify.

The moonless sky revealed stars in a Southern Hemisphere pattern that I was not used to — no Big Dipper, no North Star. It was clear and breezy, and the songs began to follow the rhythm of the ocean. Then in the shallows around the rocks, I began to see the faint, blue-green glow of luminescent algae. It would not have been visible if the lights had been on.

The harmonies continued for a long time, and when they stopped, I was provided with a candle to find my way back to my room. In the dark, I never saw the faces of my new friends, but I will never forget their gift to me on a dark night in Samoa.[9]

As this experience illustrates, it can be difficult to appreciate another culture's perspective on time. But the rewards are well worth the effort.

CHAPTER 8
How Do We Deal with Status?

Achievement   **STATUS**   Ascription

Question 5: How do we deal with status?

- Who is granted status?
- How is status earned?
- What is the social distance between high-status and low-status individuals?

Humans bring order to their worlds by creating hierarchy. In most societies, a parent has greater status than a child. A religious leader has more status than a parent. A political leader has more status than a parent or, perhaps, a religious leader. In other words, one type of person is more important than another.

Look at any tribe, team, religion, class, neighborhood, or work organization, and you will see a hierarchy. Some hierarchies are created by role, position or class, while others are created by behavior. In a classroom, the "good" students sit in the front row. In a church, the "good people" are on time and sit in the front. In certain tribes, the "good" people have beards or shave their heads. "Good" people graduate from college, "better" people get master's degrees, and the "best" people get PhDs or other advanced degrees.

Hierarchies can even appear in the advice people give each other. "Marry a doctor," a mother always says. "Marry someone from your church, tribe, or region," suggests an uncle. Statements like these show who a culture thinks is important.

All cultures establish hierarchies that determine status. The details of those hierarchies depend on whether a culture is achievement oriented (Peach) or ascription oriented (Coconut).

Achievement-Oriented Peaches

In achievement-oriented cultures, status is determined by individual accomplishments; put another way, status is earned. Peach cultures tend to be achievement oriented because accomplishments are measured by compliance to rules. In turn, accomplishments are certified by society in the form of college degrees, titles, or other individual successes.

Since achievement comes from following the rules, it is helpful to know what the rules are so one can gain a higher status if desired. This mindset is apparent in the common ritual of a speaker introduction. In the introduction, for example, a speaker may be described by the number of businesses she has started, the number of books she has written, and what degrees she has earned from prestigious universities. (*Prestigious* is another word that signals a recognized hierarchy). In the listeners' minds, all of these achievements indicate that the speaker must know what she is talking about.

In Peach cultures, people care less about where you come from or who your parents might be than about where you received your college degree and what kind of work you did to earn it. In achievement-oriented cultures, someone who has the discipline to complete a program (i.e., to follow the rules) and earn recognition is seen as accomplished.

For instance, university professors work in a highly rules-oriented achievement culture. If you were to chat with a group of professors, they could probably be persuaded to talk about their degrees, the honors they have earned, their publications, and the professional societies to which they belong. If you looked up the professors' résumés and asked them about specific presentations and publications, it would likely endear you to those professors in such a way that you would receive special attention.

As another example, if you go into your doctor's office, you will often see diplomas displayed on the wall, indicating the level of achievement that the doctor has reached. To determine if he or she is a good doctor, you do not ask about his or her hometown or tribal affiliation. You are generally only concerned with his or her performance in medical school.

Other ways to achieve in Peach cultures are less obvious than degrees or awards but are just as real. Why does someone buy a luxury car when a similar version of the car is one-third the price? The answer is that car manufacturers market using achievement appeal. Because a luxury car is far too expensive for most people to afford, being able to have one is a symbol of high achievement. The same can be true for a house, a boat, or even photos on Facebook designed to show people that you have a good life because you have done "good things."

Achievement in a Peach culture, however, can come in a variety of forms and does not always correspond to having formal education or strictly adhering to standard processes. Many Peaches pave their own roads to success. Bill Gates and Steve Jobs are good examples of this kind of achievement.

Ascription-Oriented Coconuts

On the other hand, Coconut cultures value relationships over rules. Thus, status is granted based on one's affiliation with privileged groups. These groups may be based on age, gender, family, socioeconomic class, tribe, professional guild, neighborhood, gang affiliation, religious sect, or some other characteristic. Being seen as a high-status person is very important in Coconut cultures, and it is why immigrants often have a hard time integrating into these societies. In Peach cultures, a person is respected for his or her knowledge, academic training, and measurable successes. But in Coconut cultures, a person is respected for his or her group memberships.

For example, in one Latin American town, the high-status people lived on the hill above the town, the middle-status people lived at the base of the hill, and the low-status people lived along the nearby river. However, while the houses on the hill did tend to be nicer than those in other parts of the town, the middle-status people were generally better off financially than the high-status people. So what determined status in this town? The community had long perpetuated the idea that living closer to the church was better, and the church was located on top of the hill. Thus, those living close to the church had higher status. Because of that status, they were more often called upon for duty in the church, more likely to hold elected office, and more educated.

Coconut cultures maintain their focus on status even if certain privileged groups no longer exist in their societies. For instance, France abolished its monarchy and nobility over two hundred years ago. However, coauthor Scott Hammond, who lived in France as a child, describes the ascription-oriented culture that still exists there:

> I was riding in a car with my friend Herve and his mother [Madame] outside Paris, and Madame stopped the car at the head of a tree-lined street. At the end of this street was a villa, and in front of the villa were two security guards. Madame said, "The person who lives in that villa would be the king of France today if we didn't still have that crazy president, and Herve would be in his court."
>
> Later, Herve attended the most prestigious business school in France. He has had a wonderfully successful career. He is wealthy and well educated. But none of those accomplishments bring him the status that he gets by being "in line for a title."[10]

Similarly, in the Coconut cultures of the Middle East, long conflicts have been fought between various groups. Peaches often wonder why these groups cannot simply bury the past and get along. These struggles make more sense when one understands the importance of historical ascription in these societies. To most Coconuts, a member of an enemy group will always be seen as an enemy, regardless of whether he or she has personally wronged the Coconut.

Not all Coconut cultures were once monarchies or tribal societies. Some group affiliations, in fact, are based on achievement. A well-known consultant graduated with a doctorate from Stanford University. Working on the East Coast of the US, he often encountered graduates from the Harvard Business School. He noticed that in the first meeting of difficult negotiations, the negotiating teams would often put their hands on the table in an inconspicuous way so that others could see their class rings. Finally the consultant figured out that this was an indirect way to determine who in the room was wearing a class ring from Harvard. The Harvard graduates trusted each other even if they were negotiating from different sides. The consultant's Stanford ring, however, did not bring the same kind of ascribed status.

In Coconut cultures, work performance is less important than age or work experience in determining who is in charge.

A Peach plant manager in China hired a number of local workers to build a manufacturing plant. Each of the workers had been carefully trained. Over time, several workers were identified as leadership material and were asked to assume leadership roles at the plant. To the plant manager's surprise, all of them refused. Instead, they deferred to older or more senior employees, asking if those colleagues could be made managers instead. The plant manager indicated that the senior employees' work performance was not nearly as good as that of the younger workers. But this did not matter to the younger employees; they wanted their senior colleagues to be their managers.

Coconuts often act to preserve something called face. This practice, known as saving face, is one of the most widely articulated concepts of culture. Put simply, people are said to be saving face when they act to protect their relationships, social statuses, reputations, prestige, or dignity. Since relationships matter more than rules to Coconuts, if the relationships that the Coconut values most are damaged by rules, words, or actions, the Coconut loses face. In turn, losing face means losing status in a group or organization. Thus, the price of losing face can be extreme for a Coconut.

Bert Brown[11] says that the issue of face is most prominent in business negotiations. He notes, "In some instances, protecting against loss of face becomes so central an issue that it swamps the importance of the tangible issues at stake and generates intense conflicts that can impede progress toward agreement and increase substantially the costs of conflict resolution." In other words, if the Coconuts in a negotiation fear a loss of face, their focus on saving face can hijack the discussion and make it much harder to come to an agreement.

Face saving is often associated with Asian cultures, but concepts of saving face and preserving status are found in every culture, including Peach cultures. These practices are most prominent, though, in Coconut cultures. For example, it is telling to examine the many verbs in the Chinese language that relate to saving face. (Note that directly translating the word *face* between Chinese and English is problematic.) Lin Yutang[12] notes that in Chinese, face can be

- "granted" (*liu mianzi* (留面子) or to "grant face; give (someone) a chance to regain lost honor");
- "lost" (*shi mianzi* (失面子) or to "lose face");
- "fought for" (*zheng mianzi* (爭面子) or to "fight for face"); and
- "presented as a gift" (gei mianzi (給面子) or to "give face; show respect (for someone's feelings)").

The extent to which face-saving practices are essential to Coconut cultures is illustrated by a recent experience of one of the authors. A large Asian firm requested that several companies submit a competitive bid to provide a training program to the firm. The author had a deep and long-standing consulting relationship with the firm, and his company submitted a bid because of that relationship. Much work went into completing the bid, and the author was told that a decision would be reached by a certain deadline. That deadline came and went, and no word was given. In conversations held after the deadline, representatives of the firm pretended not to know the status of the bid.

Later, it became evident that the firm had chosen another bidder and was keeping the author in the dark. When confronted, one representative simply said, "Oh, I did not want you to have to give your partners the bad news." In other words, the representative was protecting the author from having to deliver news that might cause a loss of face.

Self-Assessment: Achievement Oriented or Ascription Oriented?

By now, you may be getting a sense of whether you are achievement oriented or ascription oriented. To determine your category more specifically, fill out the table below by circling the option from each pair that best describes your preference *most of the time*. The results are nonscientific, but they are sufficient to trigger the self-examination required to establish Culture3 Dialogue.

As you complete this self-assessment, remember that most people are proud of both their accomplishments and their affiliations. In college, for example, we greatly value accomplishment, granting degrees to everyone who meets the required qualifications. But we also have fraternities and sororities that grant social status to those who belong.

Achievement   **STATUS**   Ascription

I prefer:	
When people use my title	When people say where I am from
To rely on my expertise	To rely on my connections
To trust the experienced	To trust those in charge
To have a diverse team	To work with people like me
When people are judged by accomplishment	When people are judged by status
Performance bonus	Seniority pay
A diverse work environment	A homogeneous work environment
When facts determine action	When consensus determines action
To socialize with everyone on the team	To socialize only with my friends

If you circled more answers in the left column, you are likely a Peach (achievement oriented). If you circled more answers in the right column, you are likely a Coconut (ascription oriented).

Now that you know whether achievement or status is a higher priority for you, let's examine how to effectively work with people who value the opposite concept.

Establishing Culture3 Dialogue

In Peach cultures, credentials are very important. They often follow a person's name, such as by being printed on a business card or on a nameplate in an office. Peach managers are likely to select employees with personal accomplishments, such as college degrees, and grant them privileges that will help them with their future job performance. Individuals may also be responsible to reciprocate to their status-granting institutions. They might return to an alma mater, make donations to it and go to homecoming ceremonies there, for example.

Coconut managers, on the other hand, are more impressed by what groups or social networks their employees belong to. In Coconut cultures, people are expected to be connected and to know whom they are connected to. During meetings with Coconuts, there may be a lot of "Do you know So-and-So?" kinds of conversations in the small talk before business. These discussions may include questions that seem inappropriate to a Peach, such as inquiries about family, father, mother, tribal affiliation, and even religion.

Case Study: The Boss in Flip-Flops

Ron was asked by his boss to begin merger negotiations with a medium-sized manufacturing firm headquartered in Singapore. As a recent graduate of a prestigious university in the US, Ron relied on both his law degree and his MBA to do the preliminary work on an acquisition.

Later, Ron arrived in Singapore and settled into his luxury hotel. He secured the services of a limousine and a driver and got the address of the person he was to meet, who also happened to be the hotel's owner, with whom he had a meeting planned for the next day. In the sweltering humidity, Ron's suit and starched shirt stuck to his skin, so he was glad he had chosen an air-conditioned car. He imagined that he would be meeting the owner in one of the many air-conditioned high-rise buildings in downtown Singapore. After all, the owner had several businesses and a net worth of several hundred million dollars. Certainly he would have an office to match his status.

So Ron was a little surprised when he was asked to come to the owner's home. Still, he assumed that the owner was trying to show hospitality by bringing Ron to his house. So when the limo stopped in front of a middle-class home in a lower-middle-class neighborhood, Ron thought he was at the wrong address. The brownish stucco house was mostly open, with no air-conditioning units in sight. The streets around the house were crowded.

There was a man standing in the street in what appeared to be his pajamas, with flip-flops on his feet and a New York Yankees hat on his head. He was talking and laughing with his neighbors and yelling at the street merchants as they pulled their carts of vegetables past. He had a silver-capped front tooth that sparkled as he smiled, and as soon as he saw Ron, he came up and extended his hand. "Are you Ron?"

"Yes," Ron said, not able to hide the surprise in his voice. *This* was the multimillionaire owner he had come to see?

"Welcome to my neighborhood," said the owner. "This is where it all started for me." He pointed out the old building that had housed his first plant and then gestured toward where his cousins and parents lived. "This is my world," he said. "And these are my people."

In the weeks that followed, Ron spent many hours on the front porch of the owner's house amid the heat and the blaring noise of traffic, completing one of the most difficult negotiations of his career. "This man knew everything about the business he [had] built," said Ron. "And he had never set one foot in college."

CHAPTER 9
How Do We Approach Our Work?

Specific   **FOCUS**   Diffuse

Question 6: How do we approach our work?

- Do we start with the context or with a specific point?
- Do we view projects from a wide angle or from a close-up?
- Is work integrated with or separate from our personal lives?

Two managers were assigned to complete a smaller part of a global product launch. Specifically, they were to handle certain research and product-development tasks. Each manager was given part of the assignment, the necessary deadlines, and a team to work with.

The first manager brought her team together and showed them the plans for the whole project. She then brought in a group from management and had them explain to her team members the context in which they would be working.

The second manager divided his team by area of expertise. He carefully examined what each person would need to do to be successful, and he set up training to "fill in the experience gaps." He split up the assignments and set deadlines. All completed work flowed to his assistant and then to him.

Both managers completed their portions of the project successfully and on time. In evaluations, the first team was praised for integrating their work well with other parts of the project. Some members of this team went on to lead other teams in the next generation of the product launch. The second team was praised for being technically competent and precise. Some members of this team who had developed technical expertise became technical leaders in the company.

The specific-diffuse dimension of culture measures how deeply people get involved in each other's lives. Specific (Peach) cultures view life as being separated into compartments (work, family, leisure, etc.), and people typically do not interact in more than one compartment. Diffuse (Coconut) cultures view all aspects of life as being interconnected, and interactions are not limited to particular circumstances. While these mindsets and behaviors may seem unrelated to business, they have an interesting consequence for work habits: the type of focus in a culture affects which part of a project an employee or team prefers to tackle first.

Specific Peaches

Peach cultures tend to be specific. Business projects are seen as collections of compartmentalized tasks. When a Peach team begins a project, they first focus on the details of the assignment and assign people with individual expertise to accomplish specific tasks. The team leader has the power to manage and direct the other team members, but that is the extent of his or her authority.

This is because people's lives also tend to be compartmentalized in Peach cultures. Relationships at work often stay quite separate from those at home and after hours. Coworkers, even those who spend more time together than with their families and friends, are often guarded about sharing details of their personal lives. A person's ability to perform at work is judged by how well he or she follows the rules of the workplace. Put another way, one's personal life is largely irrelevant as long as it doesn't interfere with one's ability to do one's job well. Attempts to cross these compartmentalized boundaries may be met with irritation, coldness, evasive answers, or various other behaviors that communicate, "That's none of your business." This guardedness is a deep-rooted behavior that may not even be understood by the people protecting their boundaries. To them, it may simply feel uncomfortable to receive inquiries about their personal lives.

In addition, Peach cultures tend to have independent principles and consistent moral stances. Technical standards are set by professional bodies or the applicable industry and are not project specific. Thus, they are not based on any relationship and are assumed to be fixed and immovable. Ethical standards are also fixed and defined, much like the rules in a universalist perspective. To further manage risks and build trust, Peach cultures use legal documents, requests for proposals, project plans, etc. Once established, these additional external standards are seen as binding, and violating them can have severe consequences.

In the opening story of this chapter, the second manager began with direct, focused instructions to his team. This pattern is typical of Peach cultures. Peaches like having specific instructions on how to get things done, so the second manager's teammates appreciated his exactness. Later, during regular check-ins with the team, his communication was purposeful, precise, definitive, transparent, and even blunt. He maintained a specific role: the manager of processes and the distributor of information. He did not want his team members to get bogged down with the big picture; he wanted them to focus on details.

This manager had earned his position by doing solid, detail-oriented work. He had gained the respect of his team members not only through his abilities but for having graduated to the larger, more-strategic and more-integrative parts of a project. "You start at the bottom and work your way up," he would say. Even this statement demonstrates the specificity of Peach culture: a successful person, it is assumed, starts with one set of tasks ("the bottom") and then moves on to the next set and then the next as he or she gains experience ("work your way up").

Diffuse Coconuts

Coconut cultures, on the other hand, tend to be diffuse. Professors, for instance, are treated by their students not only as instructors in the classroom but also as influential figures in other parts of the students' lives. Boss-subordinate relationships usually are not limited to office life; bosses are likely to have influence in aspects of employees' personal lives. Because of the importance of loyalty and the multilayered nature of human bonding in diffuse cultures, companies in these societies tend to have lower turnover and employee mobility.

In the story that began this chapter, the first manager began by giving her team a tour of the project. She took a wide-angle, holistic approach, giving her team members the context into which their project needed to fit. This pattern is typical of Coconut cultures. Their conversations are indirect and circuitous and may seem to wander without aim. The teammates build relationships with each other and create informal relationships with people outside their group. Overall, their communication seems evasive and ambiguous—until they understand the full context and function of the project.

Some Coconut cultures have a phrase that says (in one way or another), "Go slow to go fast." This mindset has to do with both grasping context and establishing trust through building relationships in a variety of settings. This relationship building may include spending time in settings that cross into what Peach cultures would consider personal space, such as traveling together, having a casual breakfast, talking late into the night over drinks, singing karaoke, learning about and meeting one another's significant others, or even staying in one another's homes. All these activities are meant to test the waters, to observe behaviors, to triangulate relationships, and to establish deep connections. For some Coconuts, this behavior may be a way of managing risks. Once the relationship has become comfortable and enough trust has been established, things like project scope, project-plan details, and the like can be worked out through discussion and may evolve over time. No formal contract or legal document is considered necessary. Because it is expected that well-founded relationships can endure a variety of challenges, Coconuts have confidence that future problems can be managed.

Coconut team leaders have a peer relationship with their teams and see the leader's role as one of sharing information rather than of guarding people from information overload. These leaders bend and even break rules to get projects done because they see performance standards as purely project based. While external technical standards are acknowledged, what is right for the project is the guide.

Because of the relationship orientation of Coconut teams, their members are often seen as being strong integrators and collaborators. Within a team, specific members are seen as having good technical skills and being detail oriented.

Specific and Diffuse Professions

Though specific and diffuse are cultural orientations, one can also see these dimensions within professions. Artists and strategists often start by getting the big picture (Coconut), while engineers and actuaries typically start by examining specific problems (Peach). Most of the time, both methods are needed to successfully solve complex problems.

However, each profession has within it an orthodoxy that dictates the starting point. Western medicine, for example, is largely specific in its approach to healing and has been very successful in curing specific diseases. Eastern medicine has a more diffuse approach, and its methods can prevent and even resolve some health issues that have confounded Western medicine.

Case Study: Surprised by a Project

A small US (Peach) software company came into contact with a large Japanese (Coconut) firm that was interested in the software company's specialized services. From the software team's perspective, the relationship did not seem to be going anywhere fast, but they were patient. They proactively kept in touch and responded warmly when their Japanese contacts reached out. After about two years of this, the software company suddenly received a $2 million deposit in its bank account. There was no contract or real warning, yet this is how the software team learned that they had been awarded a new project by the Japanese firm. The software team was rewarded for its ability to develop a well-rounded relationship with the Japanese managers over time.

Case Study: Too Much Management?

David, a Peach, was just trying to be helpful. He had a new team with an old mission in a market he knew. Besides, leaders lead. So he gathered the team together and gave them their marching orders: "First, connect with . . . Then . . . After that . . . If you successfully do that, then you will be able to . . . Finally . . ."

During this meeting, David expected his team members to take notes or listen carefully. He focused on explaining how to get the project done. In his mind, he was telling them the best way to do their jobs, and he expected appreciation for his wisdom and direction. Instead, his Coconut team did not listen closely, and once David left the room, they whipped up a pile of criticisms that they laid at his boss's feet. "David is a micromanager," they complained. "He holds the reins too tightly. He is a control freak."

"We are professionals," said one team member. "We know how to figure this one out for ourselves. We don't need management dictating every little step. Doesn't David trust us?"

The project ended up being a disaster. The team did exactly what David wanted. They radically complied with his method, and nothing worked. Nothing.

A little wiser, and a lot beaten up, David took a new approach for the second project with this team. He managed less. He gave a good description of the desired outcome, then said, "You are the professionals. You know how to make it happen. Come to me if you need help or additional resources." This approach led to much better results. The second project came in on time and under budget.

Self-Assessment: Specific or Diffuse?

By now, you may be getting a sense of whether you are specific or diffuse. To determine your category, fill out the table below by circling the option from each pair that best describes your preference *most of the time*. The results are nonscientific, but they are sufficient to trigger the self-examination required to establish Culture3 Dialogue.

As you complete this assessment, remember that everyone likes to get things done. We all have pressure to be productive. However, this cultural dimension is not about productivity. It is about what part of a problem you begin with. Do you zoom in or out? Do you start with a set of instructions to your team about how to do something, or do you tell your team what the outcome should be and let them find the best path?

| Specific | FOCUS | Diffuse |

I prefer:	
Instructions that are direct	Instructions that include context
To focus on my own assignment	To know what others are doing
To stay with one specialty	To be able to step in for others
Being responsible for my own domain	Sharing a domain with others
Working specific hours	Working until the work is done
A boss who gives direct orders	A leader who asks my opinion

An external set of standards	A set of standards based on the project
One right way	Many right ways
That my work is separate from my personal life	That my work is my life
Clear deadlines	Flexible deadlines

If you circled more answers in the left column, you are likely a Peach (specific). If you circled more answers in the right column, you are likely a Coconut (diffuse).

With this understanding of how you approach your work, let's examine how to effectively work with people who have a different methodology.

Establishing Culture3 Dialogue

While it is helpful to have both Peaches and Coconuts on a team, it is not uncommon for team members from one culture type to report frustration with teammates from the opposite culture type. Note that there is a high potential for conflict in this dimension of culture because it deals directly with work styles and starting points for projects. To further complicate this issue, the system of work processes is often not discussed within teams. Everyone is assumed to know the processes, and therefore they are often unspoken. In addition, a manager might believe that his or her approach to work (whether specific or diffuse) is right and suggest, directly or indirectly, that the approach of others is less efficient, less effective, or inappropriate. This tactic frequently causes offense, which in turn reduces the ability of the team to work together to achieve the desired results.

If you are a Coconut working with Peaches, your colleagues will want to start a project with clear, specific instructions about work processes, roles, and deadlines. If they do not get these details from their team leader or manager, they feel disorganized and out of place. They are less concerned with how their individual assignments fit into an overall project than with precisely what they need to do and when. Trust is more likely to be high if team members have a good relationship with a team leader who is detailed in his or her communications. Coconuts may also need to be patient with Peaches when Peaches exhibit behaviors that feel abrupt or rude. Remember that Peaches value rules over relationships, so they want to know the rules (i.e., what is expected of them) right away in order to start following them.

If you are a Peach working with Coconuts, your colleagues will want the context at the start of a project. They build trust in a leader by seeing the whole project first and then learning how they fit into the project. (To contribute to this trust, Peaches may also need to be more open than usual about their personal lives with their Coconut colleagues.) However, Coconuts do not want a leader to give them specific instructions for assignments because that makes them feel as though the leader does not trust them. Additionally, Coconuts do not want specific deadlines because they want the flexibility to divert to tasks outside their assigned areas to help others. They do believe in equifinality, which means that there are many right ways to do a project as long as they all end in the desired result.

CHAPTER 10

What Is Our Emotional Style?

Affective   **EMOTION**   Neutral

Question 7: What is our emotional style?

- How are emotions displayed?
- What is our verbal style?
- What is the value of rationalism?
- How are different ideas given weight?

An US manager was on an extended visit to his company's office in Buenos Aires, Argentina. One day, as he approached the office of an Argentinean colleague, he heard loud, highly emotional voices coming from the room. Just as he was about to go in, another Argentinean colleague stormed out, muttering insults under his breath toward his boss.

"He just does not understand," he said. "He does not understand how important this product will be!" The Argentinean continued the barrage of harsh, emotional comments, shaking his hands and clenching his fists.

Later that night, the managers met at a bar. To the surprise of the US manager, the angry employee was there as well, sitting with an arm around his boss and singing a song. Later, the Argentinean manager explained, "In our culture, emotions are quick to erupt and quick to be resolved. If we don't get publicly mad at each other at least once a month, then we are not trying very hard."

This cultural dimension does not align neatly with the two types of cultures, it is a crucial component of intercultural understanding. There are affective and neutral styles mixed among both Peach and Coconut cultures. The distinction between the two styles is simply a question of where emotion is placed during a given situation and how that emotion is appropriately displayed.

Affective and Neutral Emotional Styles

In affective cultures, emotions come quickly. Anger, frustration, and even threats are sometimes open, as are demonstrations of affection. Even strangers are included as participants or spectators in an emotional outburst. But these emotions are quickly released, and issues are quickly resolved. In fact, emotional engagement is the way caring is displayed. It is not uncommon to see Italians, for instance, in the street arguing with their friends or families. But these arguments are not destructive. They are constructive because members of affective cultures use argument and emotion to productively engage the people they care about. Just as a floral centerpiece draws the eye to it, the emotional component of conversation is central to communication.

But emotions are kept hidden in neutral cultures, taking an essential part of the communication process off the table for people from affective cultures. Still, even though neutral cultures typically keep emotions away from public view or "in the closet," those emotions are very active. When the closet is full, emotions may burst out, spilling into a conversation or encounter. On other occasions, privileged visitors are even invited to see what is in the closet. But emotions generally remain private and personal.

Affective Case Study: Too Much (or Too Little) Arguing

When one of the authors was traveling in Jerusalem, he was advised by the hotel porter to determine the cab fare with a taxi driver prior to getting into the cab. One day, the author got into a taxi with a colleague who was tired of the constant negotiation and argument about fares. The colleague told the Palestinian driver where to go and proposed a price: "One hundred dinars."

"One hundred and twenty," said the cabby. "You are taking food out of the mouths of my children at one hundred dinars."

"Okay, one hundred and thirty," said the colleague. It would be worth the extra pay for a little peace and quiet, he felt.

But the taxi driver was deeply offended. For him, negotiation of the fare was a means of social engagement. When the colleague took away the need to negotiate, he was essentially saying, "I don't want to talk to you anymore."

Neutral Case Study: Communicating in Japan

A young Latin American manager was assigned to lead a project team in Japan. Most of the team members spoke English, and the young manager was learning Japanese. Still, he complained often about the "lack of communication" within the team. "In my country," he said, "I can just look at someone on my team and almost see what they are thinking. They nod when they agree. They shake their heads when they disagree. All I get with this group is a bunch of straight-faced people, and I don't even know if they have heard me."

In Japan, as in many countries with neutral cultures, displays of emotion are subtle and reserved for insiders. Physical contact is reserved for close friends and families. Silence and subtle facial expressions are often used to communicate. Emotions are typically dammed up and held back for long periods of time before erupting like a volcano after some apparently minor provocation.

Case Study: Affective-Neutral Misunderstandings

One of the coauthors once observed a negotiation between US and Japanese firms. After a long period of socialization, the Japanese firm sent a small delegation of middle managers to the US to finalize the agreement. These managers had not been involved in the initial socialization activities. None of them had a great deal of experience in the US, nor could they speak English well. Translators were employed, but they provided only very precise translations. After two days of frustrating negotiations, the US managers complained that the Japanese managers did not care about this important business partnership. "Just look at their faces," said one US manager. "They don't want to be here."

It is true that Japanese managers often come into a business meeting with stony faces. They do not make small talk or talk about their personal lives. In this case, they had been assigned to close a business deal, and they cared a great deal about it. Their lack of emotion was seen by the US team as a lack of caring. But for the Japanese managers, it was their way of showing commitment to the details of the business transaction.

Note that while Japanese culture is clearly neutral, US culture is not radically affective. Italian, Latin American and Chinese cultures, for example, are generally much more affective than US culture. People from the US are somewhere in the middle of the spectrum.

Case Study: Two Managers

One of the authors once worked for a manager who was referred to as a "poker player." One could never tell by his face whether he was happy or sad, in a good mood or in a bad mood. He would often come into work and go right into his office and sit down. He would then call his subordinates in one by one and issue instructions for the day. He was highly process oriented and gave clear and rational instructions. If a subordinate fell short of his expectations, then he would tell that person directly and expect that person to provide a plan for meeting his expectations. This manager had a neutral style.

After six months, another manager with a completely different style replaced the original manager. The new manager would come in the door in the morning and walk around to everyone's desk. He would give his subordinates slaps on the back, high-fives, or even hugs. He would talk about everything but work, including sports and other popular topics. He would never call someone into his office unless he was angry. About every week or two, he would get into a bad mood and lapse into emotional outbursts and anger. Sometimes he would deal out firings and punishment during these moods. But he would also give apologies, hugs, and high-fives. This manager had an affective style.

Self-Assessment: Affective or Neutral?

By now, you may be getting a sense of whether you are affective or neutral. To determine your category more specifically, fill out the table below by circling the option from each pair that best describes your preference *most of the time*. The results are nonscientific, but they are sufficient to trigger the self-examination required to establish Culture3 Dialogue.

Remember that your preferences for this particular cultural dimension may be difficult to assess. But key questions can help uncover the motives behind actions and help you to see yourself. Do you think before you have physical contact with someone, or is physical contact immediate and spontaneous (like a hug, a slap on the back, or even a kiss)? When making decisions, is your first concern rationality ("Does this make logical sense?") or emotion ("How will I or others feel about this?")? Do you feel a need to apologize for your emotions, or do you see them as appropriate and a normal part of communication?

I prefer:	
To hug or embrace my colleagues	To limit all physical contact
To be spontaneous	To be deliberate
To be open with emotions	To be open with rationality
Continuous, fast-paced conversation	Silence between important ideas
Heated, animated conversation	Subtle, respectful conversation
Strong facial expressions	Cool, self-possessed expressions
High touch	High distance
Using my hands to communicate	Using my mouth to communicate
Giving feedback	Withholding feedback
Quickly forgetting anger	Storing anger

If you circled more answers in the left column, you are likely affective. If you circled more answers in the right column, you are likely neutral. Remember that this dimension is not tied to a particular culture type. Both Peaches and Coconuts can be affective, and both Peaches and Coconuts can be neutral.

With this understanding of your emotional style, let's examine how to effectively work with people who have a different style.

Establishing Culture3 Dialogue

It is not uncommon for people from affective cultures to see people from neutral cultures as being cold and distant. Similarly, it is not uncommon for people from neutral cultures to see people from affective cultures as wild and emotionally out of control. Obviously, neither viewpoint is conducive to effective teamwork.

If you have a neutral manager, understand that his or her lack of emotion does not mean that he or she is disinterested, bored, or stupid. When dealing with a neutral manager, a well reasoned argument is favored over an emotional one, so it is a good idea to communicate in writing. Avoid warm and expressive behaviors, which will likely be interpreted as a lack of emotional control and respect for the manager. Furthermore, a neutral manager is likely to be process oriented. You'll be expected to make rational arguments and stick to the point in communication. Feedback will come in the form of a rational argument or within the confines of a formal performance assessment. With a neutral manager, you may learn to see small clues that will eventually help you know whether the manager is pleased or displeased with your work.

If you have an affective manager, he or she is more likely to openly express goodwill and to respond to your work in an appreciative and warm fashion. Avoid being remote and ambiguous. Cool, detached employees will be seen as uncaring. An affective manager is also more likely to have emotional outbursts that include profanity or histrionics. Learn tolerance for these episodes, which at times may seem personal. While some people may find this behavior demeaning, being included in emotionally driven feedback is often a sign that you are part of the in-group. Interestingly, affective managers will often gauge your commitment to the organization by how willing you are to advocate for a particular approach to a problem. Affective managers don't care as much about your actually *being* right as they care about your willingness to *argue* for what you think is right.

CHAPTER 11
Transcending Difference
Through Culture3 Dialogue

After examining the seven dimensions of culture, you may feel a bit overwhelmed. How, you might wonder, can anyone possibly navigate the complexities of intercultural teams? These feelings are normal, but the good news is that they can be overcome. The story of modern South Africa demonstrates that it is possible to build Culture3 Dialogue even under the worst of circumstances.

Case Study: From Colonization to Multiculturalism

Today's multiethnic South Africa proudly claims the title of Rainbow Nation as a way to represent a shared commitment to both celebrating differences and transcending those differences. South Africa serves as a model for dialogue and community problem solving, but it also has a deep history of conflict.

South Africa was already a land rich in tribal African cultures when it was colonized by the Dutch in the 1600s and then the English in the late 1800s. Then traditions of rule by the minority whites grew to the point where an oppressive regime formalized apartheid in 1948. That system, based on a racial class structure, served to restrict land ownership, free movement, employment, participation in church and state, and other parts of life for native Africans (blacks) and forced immigrants from Pakistan, Malaysia, and other countries (known as coloreds). For much of the second half of the twentieth century, apartheid was under attack by internal revolutionary groups and international pressures. The system finally fell in 1994, presenting tremendous challenges for healing, forgiveness, and cultural bridge building.

South Africa's profound political and social history formed great chasms among the cultures of its various races. White South Africans are generally of English or Dutch lineage. Each of the black South African tribes has its own culture and values. Zulu culture is different from Xhosa culture, which is different from Sotho culture, and so on. In addition, the "colored" population includes forced and voluntary migrants from Malaysia, Indonesia, India, Pakistan, and other former Dutch and British colonies. In other words, South Africa is a country and culture made up of both Peaches and Coconuts.

This mixed cultural makeup has led to conflict throughout South African history. The British and Dutch colonizers (Peaches) came from universalist cultures. In their minds, there were rules that applied to everyone and had to be obeyed. The people of African and Asian heritage (Coconuts) came from particularist cultures, where relationships were more important than rules. As tensions arose between the colonizers and the colonized, those in power (Peaches) became increasingly more focused on oppressive rules, forcing blacks and coloreds to carry identity cards when they traveled to work. In addition, the oppressors attacked relationships by forcing fathers to work outside their homelands, away from their families.

The cultural differences continued even after the end of apartheid. White South Africans were and are monochronic, following strict schedules amidst a polychronic society in which tradition and culture were and are more flexible. White culture is more achievement oriented, placing value on education and career accomplishments. However, apartheid also included a radical ascription system, recognizing the achievements of only those from the "appropriate" race. Black Africans, on the other hand, come from tribal societies, and South Africans of Asian descent value ascription. These groups determine social status by tribal or ethnic-group affiliation and loyalty. Each tribe or group attributes status to the elderly, determines appropriate roles for men and women, and defines roles within the family. The seven dimensions of culture all look profoundly different in each major segment of South African society.

After the fall of apartheid, a great deal of ideological, practical, and cultural bridge building began and is continuing today. This huge undertaking is and will always be a central part of South Africa's social dialogue. Descendants of both colonists and colonized, natives and (relative) newcomers have learned to talk about differences and draw value from them. In the ongoing conversation, a phrase that honors both Peach and Coconut cultures has emerged. It states, "I am because we are."

Although most of us will not be confronted with South-African-scale challenges, this phrase and the word *Ubuntu* offer insight as we move toward understanding and using Culture3 Dialogue to transcend differences and build bridges.

Ubuntu

The translation of *Ubuntu* (/ʊˈbuːntʊ/ *uu-boon-tuu*; Zulu pronunciation: [ùɓúntʼú])[13] is "human kindness," but it can also be translated as "humanity towards others." For South African liberation leader and president Nelson Mandela, *Ubuntu* was a practical and profound philosophy of "the belief in a universal bond of sharing that connects all humanity."[14] From that shared bond, Mandela believed it possible to unify a nation through dialogue.

After the fall of apartheid, *Ubuntu*—advocated by Mandela and other prominent leaders, such as Bishop Desmond Tutu—became not just popularized but utilized. Author Michael Onyebuchi Eze says that the heart of *Ubuntu* is that a person is, in fact, a person because of and through other people. His idea of connection as essential to one's identity offers a way to transcend the divides between individualism and collectivism, universalism and particularism. Eze says, "We create each other and need to sustain this otherness creation. And if we belong to each other, we participate in our creations: we are because you are, and since you are, definitely I am. The 'I am' is not a rigid subject, but a dynamic self-constitution dependent on this otherness creation of relation and distance."[15]

In the wake of apartheid's fall, there were simmering and active conflicts between many communities and cultures. Often these conflicts ended up in the courts. According to Judge Colin Lamont, *Ubuntu* was used to bridge broken relationships between people and communities. He said, "*Ubuntu* favors the [reestablishment] of harmony in the relationship between parties and that such harmony should restore the dignity of the plaintiff without ruining the defendant."[16] Lamont also argued that *Ubuntu* opens space for ongoing dialogue to bridge differences.

The idea of *Ubuntu* is at the core of this book. While each dimension of culture helps us highlight and understand differences between individuals and cultures, *Ubuntu* shows us that the real project is in building bridges between those differences. Of course, it is essential to understand differences before we try to bridge them. That is why the preceding chapters of this book are important. But talking about and understanding differences alone does not lead to bridge building. Questions of cultural difference and the challenges they represent are permanent and ongoing.

While the common language provided in previous chapters serves as a good starting point, we now turn to the basic skills of creating

Culture3 Dialogue. This kind of communication allows us to take our understanding of cultural differences one step further and build bridges based on the idea of *Ubuntu*, allowing those involved to harness cultural differences and use them for mutual benefit.

Traditional Dialogue

In traditional Western organizations, it is common to seek mutual understanding through dialogue. Bridge building in a diverse group, the thinking goes, will emerge if those involved go through the process of deep self-examination paired with a thoughtful effort to understand others who are different. In this model, participants address two of the three questions involved in any successful cultural encounter (see chapter 1):

- "What do these people see when they see me?"
- "What do I see when I see you?"

When organizations do the work to understand differences, everyone in the group better understands each other's perspectives, an essential prerequisite to bridge building and problem solving. Unfortunately, organizations often find that merely achieving this understanding does not help the group members transcend differences, nor does it lead to solutions that everyone feels invested in. Instead of synergy, participants often resort to frustrated compromise; unfortunately, the deeper understanding they have achieved is that differences are deep-seated and intractable.

Regrettably, traditional dialogue predetermines this outcome because it often fails to address the third question of any successful cultural encounter: "What common ground can we stand on together?" Culture3 Dialogue offers a way to address all three questions and thus to begin building true bridges.

Establishing Culture3 Dialogue

Most tribally based African cultures have long traditions of bringing together people from different tribes to collaborate and address shared challenges. These traditions include taking the time to get to know the participants, creating a safe space for disagreement and agreement, and creating a shared vision of the ideal future.

When the same ingredients are present, workgroups are able to build a new transcendent and shared culture in which participants can harness differences to create powerful and innovative solutions that go beyond compromise. When group participants take the time to understand how they *are seen by* others, to understand how they *see* others, and to identify common ground and shared processes upon which to build a relationship of collaboration, they can—as a Ugandan businessman pointed out—"move forward *together*" in tackling difficult problems.

While Culture3 Dialogue offers a hopeful path forward, it is not an endeavor absent dissonance. Rather, it is a process that productively leverages differences. Culture3 Dialogue means finding the music of the "other" and bringing "us" and "them" together in a co-created cultural rhythm, producing a harmony impossible to imagine in either group alone. That process plus some other essential ingredients can lead to trust and unexpected solutions, even in the face of differing perspectives and disagreement.

Perhaps children can offer inspiration in this process of striving for the ideal of coming together. From early in their lives, children learn to interact with people who are different. On the playground, they regularly form groups, create and play games, disagree about rules and outcomes, and find ways to make things work. That pattern continues for today's generation in cyberspace, where children might play games with others on several continents and from many cultures. When conflict (whether real or virtual) occurs among children, feelings may be hurt, but eventually most children work out their differences and move forward in compromises or consensus decisions. Children become good at settling differences in ways that allow them to continue interacting. Unfortunately, they later learn from adults to see differences as more daunting and even game ending.

But the same skills learned in the playground "classroom" are important for adults. Those skills allow us to find ways to work productively with people who are different from us. As noted earlier, developing those skills requires deep self-examination and a clear understanding of others. But to create a space where self- and other-understanding can be useful—in other words, to build commitment to Culture3 Dialogue and to mutually valuable solutions—we must intentionally generate the conditions leading to the creation of common ground.

Both group leaders and group members can help to maximize everyone's contribution to the process of developing mutual understanding, growing together, and harnessing differences. This combined effort can eventually establish Culture3 Dialogue, which in turn can produce solutions at a level not yet imagined by any one individual. Three priorities are essential to help everyone in the group establish Culture3 Dialogue.

Step 1: Understand Yourself

First, focus on understanding yourself and how others might see you. Whether you are a Peach or a Coconut, you will impact other group members, particularly those who are different. Likewise, you must find a way to "hear" others, particularly those whose cultural values you might disagree with or whose approaches might rub you the wrong way. Moving beyond certainty about "one right way" and one "obvious" meaning behind an interaction will begin opening the door to Culture3 Dialogue.

If you are a group leader, a good way to start a project is to disclose your highest ambitions for the group. Tell the participants what is possible if they all come together. Help them understand that mediocrity is the highest possible achievement when working individually. Share your own cultural preferences, and provide time to discover each participant's cultural preferences and what he or she brings to the discussion. Although you may be eager to address the project at hand, discuss the importance of "sitting with" differing perspectives (rather than discounting or dismissing them) and how best that can be achieved. Finally, share ways you will help the group refocus when that highest ambition starts to get lost. Remember that as the group leader, you are responsible to help the group move forward in a positive way. Call out misunderstandings stemming from differing cultural values and suggest ways to focus on shared priorities. Highlight breakthrough moments when culture meets culture and creates something better, even something best.

If you are a group member, focus on speaking only for yourself. Most of us are particularly good at saying, "Research says . . ." or "Experts in this field believe . . ." or "The literature says . . ." when we have a strong opinion. These are efforts to speak for a broader truth, perhaps in the hope that the assertion will be accepted without question. Speaking only for oneself—that is, for the truth of one's own experiences—opens the door for others to also speak for themselves in ways that are truthful, honest, and revealing.

Try using the following statements to soften your assertions and leave space for others to share their perspectives and experiences:

- "In my culture, I have seen . . ."
- "In my experience . . ."
- "The research and data I understand says . . ."
- "From my point of view . . ."

Step 2: Make It Safe

Second, make it safe for others. We have all said something to a group or individual and not been heard (or have been misunderstood). This experience can rob us of our dignity and significance to the group. If someone instead takes the time to listen to us and then builds on what we and others have said, it enhances our dignity with the group and lets us know that we are valued and understood.

Safety requires each group member to suspend the certainty that his or her perspective or approach is "the way things should be." Whether you are a group leader or a group member, when one perspective seems to be dominating the discussion, invite those who might see things differently or hold different values to share their thoughts.

As a group leader, you can model to the group that being open minded is a way of building one side of the bridge and allowing for greater disclosure and deeper understanding. You may find it worthwhile to point out that suspending certainty does not mean that group members must give up their core cultural values or beliefs. It simply means that when those values become the center of a dispute among team members, it can be useful to set aside those ideas temporarily in search of greater understanding. Encourage group members to be cautious of asserting their cultural values and beliefs in ways that discourage others from sharing their perspectives or ideas.

As a group member, one of the most powerful ways you can make it safe for others is to listen to your own listening. Said in another way, pay attention to the way that you are hearing what others say. Are you getting angry? Are you trying to jump in too quickly without listening? Are you giving every idea full consideration? Try using the following statements to show that you are listening, that you honor what others have said, and that you want to build toward common ground:

- "I liked what you said, and it made me think about . . ."
- "Your idea triggered a thought about . . ."
- "When you said _____, I started thinking about . . ."

When teammates come from different cultures and try to find solutions to important challenges, disagreement and misunderstanding are inevitable. The way each group member handles frustration can preserve or damage hard-won safety. When you notice yourself becoming irritated, you may want to use statements like these to keep your negative feelings from getting in the way of Culture3 Dialogue:

- "One of the reasons I am feeling this way is . . ."
- "The quick/slow pace of this dialogue is not common in my culture."
- "I am frustrated because I am not used to making decisions or digesting data this quickly/slowly."
- "When you said/did _____, I took it to mean _____. Is that what you meant?"

Some frustration can arise because discussion and decision-making are happening quickly. Communication in the modern world is crowded with media noise, loud voices, and high volume. Ideas and information move so rapidly through our digitally-mediated environment that comprehension is difficult and real listening is almost impossible. Group leaders need to slow interaction down. Give people time to digest their ideas, think, ponder, and even meditate. During formal dialogue, build in periods of silence where people can think about important things that have been or should be said. To help each group member contribute to effective processing of ideas and deeper exploration of approaches, try saying things like these:

- "Let's go into a little more depth about that before we move to . . ."
- "Can we add another layer of detail?"
- "Let's think about this for a while."

Step 3: Learn as You Go

Third, focus on a process of moving forward and learning at the same time. This process is called emergence or path making.

An example of failed path making comes from the US and North Vietnam's mid-1970s efforts in Paris to negotiate the end of the Vietnam War. For eighteen months, rather than taking steps to end hostilities, the diplomatic teams argued over the shape of the conference table. Both sides reported to the media on how important it was to have the right kind of table. Meanwhile, people on both sides of the conflict continued to die. What would have happened if someone had simply said, "We don't need a table" or "We will accept a table of any shape, but let's end this conflict now"?

The Brazilian educator Paulo Freire once wrote, "You make the path by walking."[17] To make progress, your group needs to move forward. Sometimes when you walk together, you find that the shape of the table or other things that once seemed critical are no longer important. As a group leader, when your group gets sidelined by peripheral challenges, refocus everyone by reviewing the highest ambitions for the group (which you shared in step 1). You may even want to ask the group whether the path-blocking disagreement is a "table-type" debate or a debate that helps move toward that highest ambition.

The process of learning and moving forward requires the group leader and each group member to allow enough time for group identity to form. Most people who begin this process have an overly optimistic view of how long it will actually take to reach transcendence with their groups. Not only is dialogue an ongoing process, but as with anything of value, it often takes more time than expected for trust and transcendence to emerge in constructive and productive ways. Rather than seeking quick solutions to complex issues within a project, it may be useful for the group leader to invite group members to share their perspectives on facets of those issues. Such discussion will help the group get a more comprehensive understanding of the issues and how they are interrelated. More importantly, in early stages of the project, that sharing will help group members to better understand their own and others' discussion styles, cultural values, priorities, and potential areas of disagreement. Group leaders can use these early interactions to expand the number of possible solutions, especially before many ideas have emerged.

Results of Establishing Culture3 Dialogue

There is a wonderful power in having people with good intentions and strong technical qualifications come together in a constructive way for a period of time. Transcending the challenges at hand can mean discovering new and unexpected solutions, building new bridges, resolving entrenched problems, and creating outcomes exceeding the expectations of those who planned and participated in the dialogue.

This kind of result happened in a UN-recognized NGO that one of the coauthors observed. The group members gathered in Belgium from eighteen different countries to find new ways to expand the NGO's influence across the globe. After three days of working together, there was an unusual proposal: "Let's go out of business," one person said. Transcendence came as the group members realized that their international organization was, in fact, a barrier to problems that needed solutions at the local level. The group did dissolve, and local organizations with the same purpose have since flourished. It was a surprising outcome, but in terms of its impact on the desired goal, it exceeded the expectations of everyone involved.

COUNTRY REPORTS

In addition to getting clearer on how your own cultural values impact the way you engage with others on global teams, you'll want to start with a basic understanding of your teammates' cultural values. Understanding how you and your teammates might approach challenges, as defined by one or more of the cultural dimensions discussed in this book, will help you identify potential misunderstandings *and* possible synergies. Tapping into values and motivations behind behaviors offers a path to building a Culture3 Dialogue.

The country reports that follow offer our perspective on where each country falls along the Peach-Coconut continuum. Each report starts with a graphic representation of the cultural dimensions then offers highlights, history, culture, and suggestions for establishing Culture3 Dialogue. The featured countries are the first of what we hope to be a much longer list and were chosen because of their strong business relationship with the US.

In reading a country report, please remember that behaviors can vary, even within a particular culture. Use each report as a starting point. Being even slightly informed about the history, culture, and approaches to establishing Culture3 Dialogue will help you build stronger working relationships. Before moving forward though, check your understanding of your teammates' cultures and how they vary from yours by watching interactions and interpersonal dynamics around you and by talking with your teammates. You may notice that the younger generation has been influenced by global media and may have changed their behaviors as a result. In many cases, though, the underlying culture has not changed.

Good luck as you work to create stronger working relationships with your teammates.

Argentina

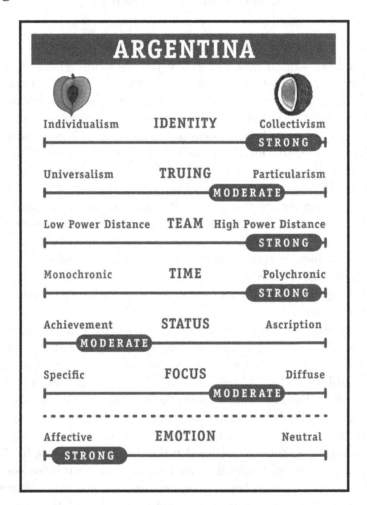

Highlights

Like most Latin American cultures, Argentinean culture demonstrates strong Coconut tendencies. Because interpersonal relationships and group cohesiveness are a priority, commitments to deadlines are more flexible, and project plans tend to lack specificity and are fairly easily altered. Responsibility and accountability are strongly linked to one's group membership. Argentineans see high power distance as an important component of effective leadership and organizational structure. Leaders are expected to be charismatic and provide a clear, strong vision. Displays of emotion run the gamut in the workplace but can be intense. Appropriate expressions of affection and frustration, for example, are an acceptable and normal part of interaction in the workplace and in negotiations.

History

Argentina has a population with mostly European ancestry, and most people live in urban areas. Much like other Latin American countries colonized by the Spanish and dominated by the Roman Catholic Church during the colonial period, Argentina inherited authoritarian and patron-client political and social structures. After the country gained its independence, autonomous *caudillos* (charismatic landowners) maintained provincial order and protected the population, reinforcing many established reciprocal relationships and consolidating the power and control of the state. While elites in political leadership positions pushed the country toward modernization, personal-loyalty networks stymied constitutional reform. From the world economic crisis in the 1930s through the end of World War II, a small group of families dominated most industrial and economic sectors in Argentina. Reform efforts alternated between military dictatorship and progress toward democracy, with a low from 1976 to 1983 that brought a reign of terror (the Dirty War) and disastrous economic administration. Since that time, Argentina has been engaged in reconstructing its economy and building a democratic government that moves beyond traditions of authoritarianism.

Culture

As in other Coconut cultures in which the state and society fail to offer a reliable structure, Argentinians tend to pursue their own self-interest, at least outside family-and-friend contexts. Argentineans also value assertiveness and see confrontation as a valuable component of negotiation. Leaders command respect and obedience through charisma and build support through extensive patron-client relationships. At the same time, Argentina's history of political schism and social and economic disruption tends to reinforce reliance on family, friend, and acquaintance networks rather than on legal frameworks. Confrontations in business contexts and in day-to-day family and friend relationships are characterized by open emotional display.

Establishing Culture3 Dialogue

Working with Argentineans requires a significant amount of effort to get through the Coconut shell. Accept uncertainty, particularly in developing and carrying out project plans. Those who expect tasks to be tightly structured may be disappointed. Invest in relationships that then lead to mutual understanding of priorities. This investment requires achieving a delicate balance: displaying strong, authoritative leadership that fits within the prevailing high-power-distance structure *and* connecting with those of equal standing. High power distance also makes it more difficult to successfully encourage lower-status individuals to risk sharing ideas that may conflict with prevailing practices.

Australia

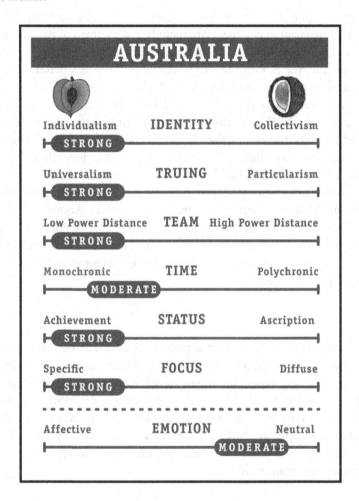

Highlights

Reflecting its British and Irish links, Australian culture holds strong Peach values. Low power distance reflects the importance of egalitarianism in Australia. Universal rules of behavior structure and govern interaction. Australians see strong pursuit of individual self-interest and performance as appropriate ways to get ahead. Educational and professional accomplishments are both important sources of status. Honoring time commitments and adhering to rules of politeness are also core values.

History

Captain James Cook took formal possession of Australia in 1770 for the UK. The ensuing colonization, including the spread of European diseases and conflict over land, resulted in many deaths among Australia's native people, the Aborigines. Established initially as a penal colony for convicts from the British realm, Australia had its identity further shaped by the discovery of gold in 1851, the formation of the Commonwealth of Australia in 1901, and the supplying of troops to fight for the UK in conflicts like the Boer War and World Wars I and II. A changing population further shaped Australia's growing independent identity. By the 1970s, Australia had become a multicultural society, including significant numbers of southern European and Asian immigrants. In redefining "Aussie" identity, Australia now counts Aboriginal culture as an essential component of its national heritage. Australians today are proud of the way in which a nation of convicts and working-class people overcame a harsh climate to establish a strong economy and an educated and egalitarian society.

Culture

Although it is derived from a history of contradiction and change, Australian culture reflects Peach values. Australians are tolerant and value fairness and equal treatment of all, even though Australian organizations are typically hierarchical. While the environment may be somewhat relaxed in work settings, civility and adherence to rules of politeness are expected. Strongly performance oriented, Australian society recognizes individual achievement more than it recognizes behavior that promotes group welfare.

Establishing Culture3 Dialogue

Work within Australia's potentially contradictory set of values. Provide a balance of inspirational leadership with efforts to not be seen as too charismatic. This means emphasizing integrity and inspiring respect from subordinates while also sending the message that you remain "one of the boys/girls." Inspiring improved performance entails balancing an egalitarian, "we're-all-in-this-together" attitude with appropriate rewards for individual achievement.

Benelux (Belgium, the Netherlands, and Luxembourg)

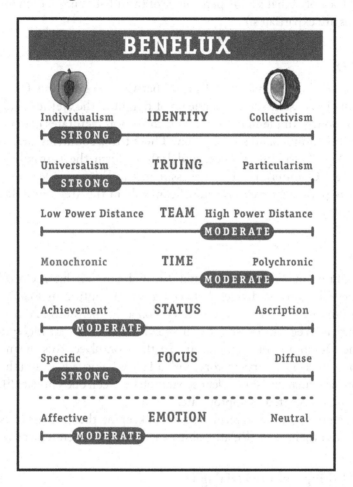

Highlights

Belgium, the Netherlands, and Luxembourg present an intriguing mix of Peach and Coconut cultures—in other words, they are CocoPeach cultures. They are moderately polychronic, more so in the countryside and less so in the cities. Citizens of all three countries are strongly committed to the idea that rules and procedures govern all interaction, regardless of one's relationships. All three countries emphasize individual effort and achievement as the most important ways to get ahead. Private life and work relationships are carefully divided. One's duties to colleagues, superiors, and subordinates do not extend beyond the "shop door." (It should be noted that a large percentage of the inhabitants of each of these nations are expatriates.)

History

Located in northwestern Europe between France and Germany, Benelux is a customs union made up of Belgium, the Netherlands, and Luxembourg. Implemented in 1944, the union facilitates cooperation around economic, and social policy. These three countries later joined with West Germany, France, and Italy to form the European Coal and Steel Community, a predecessor to the European Union (EU). Benelux plays a particularly significant role in the area of intellectual property.

Culture

Belgium, the Netherlands, and Luxembourg all have CocoPeach cultures. Belgium is divided between a Dutch culture in Flanders (in the north) and a French culture in Wallonia (in the south). As a whole, Belgium is an egalitarian society with gender equity held as a high priority.

The Dutch are also egalitarian. In the workplace, this means that decision-making is participatory, with all ideas being valued and the boss making the final decision. Clear separation between one's private life and work life is accepted as appropriate.

Luxembourgers are typically reserved, keeping their private lives separate from their work. Relationships are structured hierarchically.

Establishing Culture3 Dialogue

Develop and maintain formal and reserved relationships. Third-party introductions are valuable relationship builders, as is providing academic credentials. Be patient in building relationships, and plan for trust to be developed over time. In negotiations with Belgians, avoid direct confrontation while providing time for evidence-based, logical discussions that adequately explore alternatives. The Dutch, on the other hand, tend to be much more direct and even blunt. Across Benelux, decisions are more successful when they reflect consensus and are made after open discussions in which each participant's opinion may be heard.

Brazil

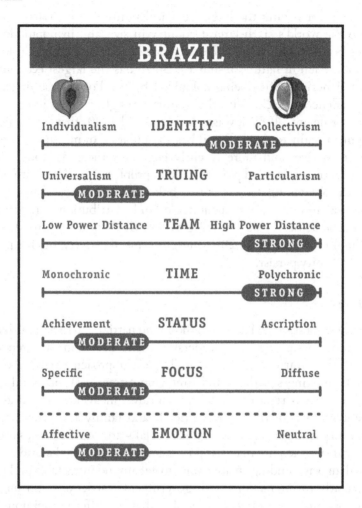

BRAZIL

Individualism	IDENTITY	Collectivism
	MODERATE	
Universalism	TRUING	Particularism
MODERATE		
Low Power Distance	TEAM	High Power Distance
		STRONG
Monochronic	TIME	Polychronic
		STRONG
Achievement	STATUS	Ascription
MODERATE		
Specific	FOCUS	Diffuse
MODERATE		
Affective	EMOTION	Neutral
MODERATE		

Highlights

As in other Coconut cultures, business in Brazil is driven much more by relationships and connections than by strict schedules and deadlines. Time is approached casually. However, Brazilians link status to individual achievement. At the same time, membership in social groups and duties that promote group welfare remain important. Leaders are expected to maintain high power distance when working with subordinates. Brazilians are comfortable with moderate expressions of emotion.

History

Known for having the largest tropical rain forest on Earth, Brazil is also the world's sixth-largest country in size and in population. It shares borders with every South American country except Chile and Ecuador. Rich in natural resources, Brazil has the largest economy in South America. After being colonized by the Portuguese, it gained independence in 1822. With the country struggling under intermittent military rule until 1985, it wasn't until the mid-1990s that economic development really took off. Brazil has a population of mixed (European, African, native, and more recently Japanese) ancestry. Today, stark economic inequality and poverty remain problematic, along with widespread problems related to crime, balancing the use and protection of natural resources, and inequitable land distribution. Brazil made significant strides while preparing to host the World Cup in 2014 and the Summer Olympics in 2016, but problems of poverty and inequality of opportunity persist.

Culture

Brazil has a strongly Roman Catholic and patriarchal society, although women are assuming more leadership roles. Brazilians are generally free-spirited, warm, and outgoing. Time is approached with a casual attitude, making schedules and time commitments flexible and often unreliable. As is typical in Coconut cultures, meals are viewed as important symbols of the value of friends and family and often happen before official business is conducted. Social status is often measured by one's ability to acquire material possessions. Brazilians take pride in the "Brazilian way," finding creative ways to get around intractable problems, particularly in interactions with government restrictions and bureaucracy. Brazilians are often comfortable sharing differing opinions and arguing passionately; relationships aren't necessarily damaged because of disagreement or dispute.

Establishing Culture3 Dialogue

Invest significant time and effort in getting to know Brazilian colleagues. This will mean that meetings may not begin on time, schedules and agendas are tentative and can be easily changed, and social interaction outside of work settings will be as important as official negotiations.

Don't rush negotiations. Since there is no strict protocol to structure meetings and negotiations, expect free-for-all discussions in which participants may interrupt each other. Given this preference for open, informal conversations, plan sufficient time to look through all details prior to signing an agreement. Avoid public confrontation with and criticism of an individual, as these behaviors cause loss of face. Because Brazilians build relationships with individuals, not with companies, maintain the same negotiation teams; changes to a team will mean starting over in developing working relationships.

Canada

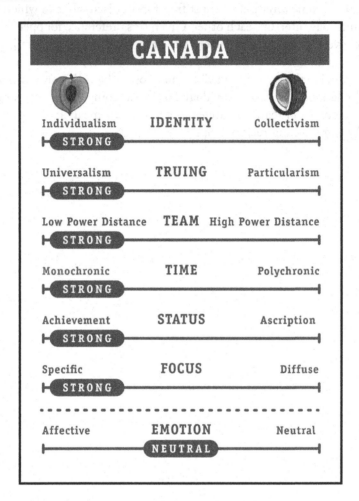

Highlights

As is typical for Peaches, Canadians see time and deadlines in a strongly monochronic fashion. Individual achievement is closely linked with self-worth and with one's status at work and in society. Canadians are deeply committed to following established rules and procedures when dealing with others, regardless of the nature of their relationships with those people. Canadians focus on individual achievement as the means to both personal and group success. Low power distance prevails between leaders and subordinates; interactions are typically relaxed, and ideas for innovation and change are seen as valuable regardless of their source. Canadians maintain clear divisions between work and their private lives.

History

Canada is the second-largest country on Earth by area and maintains one of the strongest economies in the world. Colonized initially by the French and then the British, Canada became a unified state under the Confederation Act of 1867 but retained both formal and informal ties to the UK. Constitutional reforms in 1982 kept the British queen as the head of state but ended British control over Canada. Today, Canada has a parliamentary democracy. Canada and the US have a close economic relationship, symbolized by the signing of the North American Free Trade Agreement (NAFTA) in 1993. The US consumes approximately 75 percent of Canada's exports. Canada today faces multiple critical challenges: protecting the environment while utilizing its rich natural resources, continuing its economic development, addressing indigenous populations' needs and concerns, accommodating an increasingly diverse immigrant population, and reducing poverty.

Culture

While each Canadian province has a unique history, Canadians in general share a multiculturalism derived from French, British, European, and indigenous legacies. This heritage continues to evolve as immigrants infuse Canadian culture with diverse experiences and perspectives (for example, Chinese is now the third-most-commonly spoken language in Canada, behind English and French). Canadians take pride in their nationality and in their diverse heritage. They see themselves as different (more tolerant and polite, less materialistic) from their US neighbors. Life and relationships are generally informal and not highly ritualized, although this preference varies by province. Time and punctuality are important in structuring business planning and relationships. Canadians typically pursue individualist ends.

Establishing Culture3 Dialogue

Be polite, somewhat informal, and relaxed when interacting with Canadians. Tact, diplomacy, and appeals to common sense go a long way in both negotiations and supervision of subordinates. Get down to business after minimal small talk in business meetings and negotiations. Despite the informal and relaxed atmosphere of most business meetings, Canadians value adherence to schedules and agendas. Rational, logical, and evidence-based arguments are more effective than emotional ones. All attendees at meetings are typically expected to participate, and input is valued regardless of the status of the contributor.

China

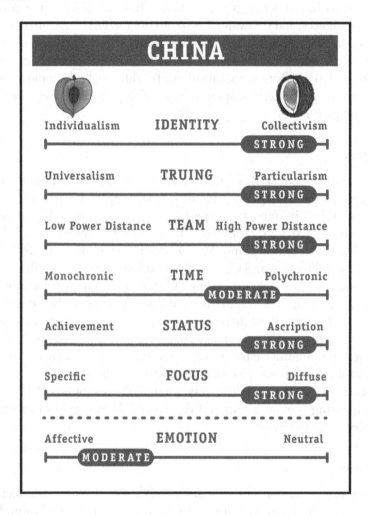

Highlights

China is a Coconut culture that has historically been heavily impacted by Confucianism. As a result, those with status often come from the "right" family, school, political party, or connections. While values are changing, Confucianism continues to structure life in powerful ways. Ascription may play a more important role than achievement in a person's position and movement within a company. By extension, relationships in a particular situation often dictate decisions, affect whom one does business with, and define ethical behavior. Business choices, the pursuit of those choices, and the evaluation of success and failure are often driven by the desire to benefit a group rather than by individual self-interest. An outsider will quickly notice the hierarchical structure and high power distance in most Chinese organizations. In addition, both employers and employees carry specific responsibilities of respect that extend beyond the workplace.

History

Situated in East Asia, China claims five thousand years of history. Chinese people take great pride in China's imperial legacy of strong leaders and in its recent emergence as one of the world's strongest economies, particularly following its loss of sovereignty to the UK in the nineteenth century and Mao Zedong's economically disastrous Great Leap Forward and Cultural Revolution campaigns in the twentieth century. Although it remains a Communist state, China now follows Deng Xiaoping's pragmatism: "It doesn't matter if the cat is black or white so long as it catches mice." This pragmatism has transformed the way state ownership, central planning, and the dominance of the Chinese Communist Party (CCP) facilitate economic growth under "red capitalism." It has also sparked questions about how to maintain a hierarchically structured society when that structure is challenged by a growing economic gap and the accompanying gaps in access to privilege and power.

Culture

In China, the concept of *guanxi* (关系)—a personal connection and the benefits gained from that relationship—is central to understanding social interaction. Confucianism explains the appropriate actions to build and maintain *guanxi*. *Guanxi* and "the good society" are achieved when hierarchical social relationships are governed by certain virtues: social order, obedience, moderation, and *renqing* (人情) (benevolent respect for the feelings of others). Relationships are defined by the position one holds; those in positions of power and those of greater age exercise authority over, and are entitled to respect from, those in lower positions and those who are younger, regardless of which group has more education or achievements. Obedience to those of position, age, or both helps to maintain both healthy organizations and a healthy country. Expectations of obedience are moderated, however, by avoidance of extremes, including public displays of emotion. Further moderation comes from the shared virtue of *renqing*, which helps to prevent inappropriate actions that would damage *guanxi*.

Establishing Culture3 Dialogue

Focus on the development of *guanxi* with Chinese counterparts. A relationship of trust is best built through showing overt respect to those in positions of power, even if a Chinese leader's training and expertise may be less than those of subordinates. Furthermore, act the part of a leader by bringing a vision of direction and providing orders for carrying out that vision. Efforts to flatten organizational procedures and structures will be less effective. For messages to resonate and truly motivate change and improvement, they should emphasize collective responsibility rather than recognize individual achievements.

Costa Rica

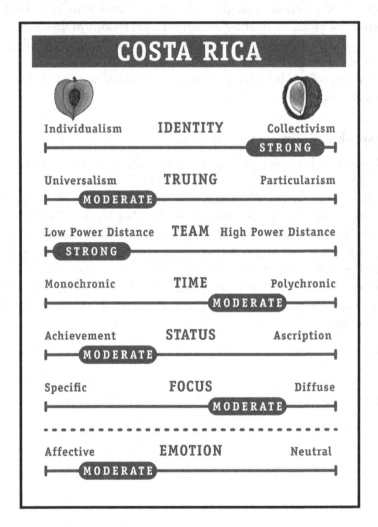

Highlights

Costa Ricans, or Ticos, exhibit both Peach and Coconut cultural traits but lean toward Coconut culture. They are moderately polychronic, allowing for flexibility in managing time and being open to shifting deadlines. Status comes from one's own efforts. At the same time, Ticos see the most value in efforts that support and promote the welfare of their social groups. Teams typically have a flat structure, with leaders maintaining low power distance. Displays of emotion in negotiations and discussions are acceptable.

History

Costa Rica is located between Nicaragua and Panama. Colonized by Spain, it became a sovereign nation in 1821. Costa Rica is committed to nonintervention internationally. Reacting to a period of falling incomes and rising prices at the end of the 1990s, Costa Rica made plans to privatize state-owned enterprises. Following widespread protest and unrest and a court ruling declaring the privatization plans unconstitutional, the government moved to support the modernization of enterprises, continuing those efforts today. Attesting to the success of those efforts, real gross domestic product (GDP) has doubled during the last generation. Costa Rica is also pursuing other progressive reforms. It elected its first female president, Laura Chinchilla, in 2010 and has committed to becoming one of the first carbon-neutral nations by 2021.

Culture

Ticos have a negative view of militarism, and they avoid confrontation in their personal interactions whenever possible. While individuality and personal privacy are important, Ticos also prize group conformity. Individuals are treated with respect regardless of status or social class. Although Costa Rica no longer designates the Roman Catholic Church as the nation's official religion and secularization is increasing, Catholicism and other Christian religions continue to influence values and behavior. Ticos are more likely to accept their fates as the will of God rather than attributing achievements to individual efforts alone.

Establishing Culture3 Dialogue

Because Ticos are typically risk averse and resist change, diplomatically find middle ground and avoid aggressive tactics aimed at "defeating your opponents." Business interaction is typically polite but informal. Presenting proposals to an entire group is appropriate, as Ticos value equality and democratic decision-making.

Finland

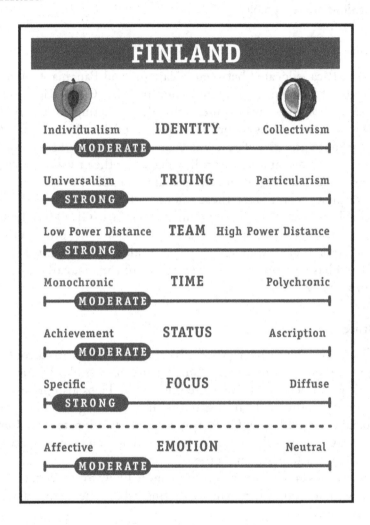

Highlights

Finland falls squarely on the Peach side of the cultural spectrum. The country is proud of its strong tradition of universalism; rules apply to everyone. Women and men are treated relatively equally, and individual rights are carefully protected. Individual needs rather than group needs motivate behavior. Finns see value in low power distance between members of society. Work relationships are generally friendly but formally structured and may not endure outside the workplace, while personal, nonwork relationships are informal and separate from work.

History

Finland achieved independence in 1917 after a long history of Swedish (1155–1809) and Russian (1809–1917) rule. Although influence from the Soviet Union continued (the Winter War led to Finland's loss of land and resources), Finland began reorienting toward Europe following World War II, joining international monetary, economic, and security organizations. Finland joined the EU in 1995 and adopted the euro as its currency in 1999. Despite this reorientation, Finland still sees itself as somewhat separate from the rest of Europe and takes pride in having one of the cleanest environments in the world. Leveraging a nearly fifty-percent income tax, Finland has a Scandinavian welfare-state system, with welfare and social security (including minimum income) guaranteed for all citizens. Enjoying strong economic growth from the end of World War II to the early 1990s, Finland later struggled with deep recession but followed Western deregulation trends. Finland has developed a strong, high-tech economy, making significant contributions to electronics and mobile communications, with notable companies like Nokia leading the way.

Culture

In the public sphere, Finns prioritize relatively equal treatment of men and women, flexible gender roles, and consensus-oriented government and management styles. Businesses are required by law to involve their employees in decisions that affect employees, their work, and their working conditions. Power distance is low, demonstrated by regular delegation of responsibility and the view that all members of a project team contribute value to achieving results. Employees expect clear definitions of responsibility and authority and the space for individual initiative within those parameters. Open office plans reflect the importance of direct and open communication.

Establishing Culture3 Dialogue

Respect the core values of open communication, low power distance, collective decision-making, and individual responsibility and initiative. To motivate performance, develop an inspiring and shared vision, clearly explain responsibilities (matched with employee capabilities), and show loyalty among different levels of management. Emphasis on individual initiative and accountability will contribute to the success of teams. Provide clear goals and take ultimate responsibility for their completion, but Finns will respond best when they are given space to find the means to achieve those goals.

France

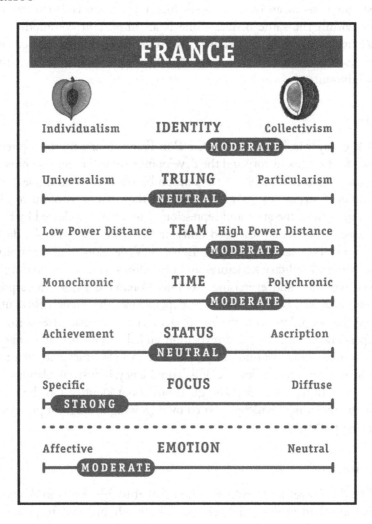

Highlights

As a CocoPeach society, France is highly regulated by rules and laws. While most accept that reality, a *débrouillard* (resourceful and smart person) knows how to get around the system when necessary. The French can be assertive and generally enjoy verbal confrontation tempered by rational argument. Moderate displays of emotion are acceptable. Although high power distance is the norm between employees and those in the upper echelons of an organization's hierarchy, there is much less distance within the same office. Time is an important commodity, but relationships can take precedence over deadlines. French society sees the preservation of French culture and its unique ways of doing things as paramount.

History

A key player in Europe today, GDP in France is among the top ten in the world. France's history and the development of its unique combination of cultural values is a story of the tension between competing ideals and institutional structures. Working through these tensions often resulted in the growth of the state and repression of resistance, followed by revolt and rejection of state-prescribed unity and control. For example, during his seventy-two-year reign, King Louis XIV developed administrative, fiscal, tax, and military structures and procedures while consolidating the centralized state and exercising absolute monarchical rule. In response to centralization, control, and state dependence, the French Revolution swung the pendulum to the values of democracy, diversity, freedom, and independence. Although this revolution ended in violence and anarchy, this tension would continue to play out in various times and areas: the Napoleonic period, Charles de Gaulle's presidency, industrial relations (collective bargaining), and ongoing questions about identity and the role of the state, including challenges posed by a growing immigrant population from North Africa.

Culture

Paths to power and privilege often run through the *Grandes Écoles*, state-controlled professional schools. These schools tend to produce a powerful and limited elite whose careers include work in the civil service, government, and business sectors. As might be expected in such a system, power distance is high. Those outside the elite circles may show an ambivalent attitude toward authority. Because of a strong social safety net and job security, the French do not have a strong future orientation. Grounded in a legacy of oscillation between extremes, the French passively submit to authority at times and aggressively assert themselves at other times. To avoid uncertainty, the French invest effort in developing deep personal relationships and building networks of support.

Establishing Culture3 Dialogue

Find a balance between respect for high power distance and the cultural changes now reducing that power distance. Understand the networks of personal relations within your company and adapt your leadership style accordingly. You may need to maintain some distance while also interacting on a more personal level that encourages team bonding around a common cause. Find ways to innovate and work creatively within extensive rules and regulations. This task requires pragmatism and the ability to respect and leverage the French values of exceptionalism and originality.

Germany

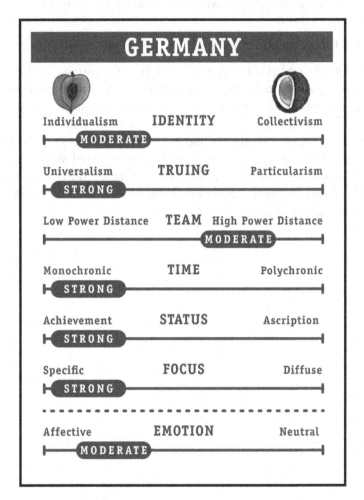

Highlights

To understand German urgency about time is to understand a key component of German behavior. Work is highly structured in Germany, which has a solidly Peach culture. Meeting deadlines, strictly honoring time commitments, maximizing efficiency, and carefully planning and executing consume much of the workday. Emphasis is placed primarily on individual achievement; efforts to improve and evaluate performance focus on the individual. Rules apply to everyone equally and come from common standards. Work relationships and private relationships are clearly divided. Since time and tasks are high priorities, work friendships are generally limited in scope.

History

Germany is one of the world's top economic performers and has the biggest economy in the EU today. Germany became a unified nation-state in 1871 as a result of a state military campaign. Following the same pattern, the state played an essential role in Germany's industrialization. As a latecomer to European imperialism and the accumulation of overseas colonies, Germany developed a romantic view of the past and was critical of modernity. After World War I, National Socialism or Nazism (grounded in other romantic ideas about obedience to state leadership) found a ready audience for its message of liberation from the hardships of reparation payments and economic difficulty. Although the Nazis were defeated in World War II, it was not until the 1960s that German youth challenged the cultural values surrounding obedience to the state. Still, the role of the state remains central as Germany grapples with European economic woes.

Culture

Given Germany's tradition of a strong, interventionist state and the uncertainty accompanying major upheavals throughout its history, Germans seek institutionalized structure and order through established rules and procedures. They value high power distance, and they focus on individual rather than group achievements, discounting group loyalty. Those values may be manifested in confrontational and assertive ways. Straightforward talk and aggressive debate are seen as productive methods of addressing issues at work. Tasks often become more important than interpersonal relations, and ideas may be presented in confrontational ways. On the other hand, expressions of emotion in public are rare, leading some to assert that Germans are difficult to get to know, skeptical, and aloof.

Establishing Culture 3 Dialogue

Align leadership practices with an understanding of acceptable and unacceptable behaviors in a predominantly Peach culture. Provide careful planning with clear deadlines and systematic assessment of performance. Assertiveness, tolerance of conflict, and effective delegating of responsibility are all important leadership traits. Straightforward discussion will also contribute to effective leadership and successful negotiations.

India

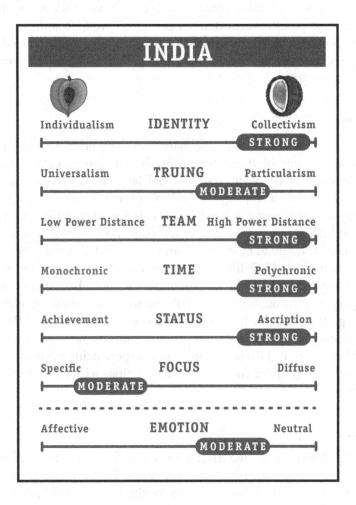

INDIA

Individualism	IDENTITY	Collectivism
		STRONG

Universalism	TRUING	Particularism
	MODERATE	

Low Power Distance	TEAM	High Power Distance
		STRONG

Monochronic	TIME	Polychronic
		STRONG

Achievement	STATUS	Ascription
		STRONG

Specific	FOCUS	Diffuse
MODERATE		

Affective	EMOTION	Neutral
	MODERATE	

Highlights

While the clock certainly structures interaction in India, particularly in urban areas, this culture approaches time in a polychronic fashion. As in other Coconut cultures, scheduled events, meetings, and projects may not go as planned and are subject to changes beyond any individual's control. India's caste system has a significant impact on status; respect for those of higher castes is expected and accepted. Reflecting the enduring importance of the family as the basic unit of Indian society, group welfare takes precedence over individual accomplishment, and personal problems are often fair game for a group to address. Indian society remains stratified. Formal structure, with appropriate social roles and privileges, determines one's position at work, and these factors are clearly understood.

History

As the second-most-populous nation in the world (behind China), India is also one of the most ethnically, religiously, culturally, and linguistically (with twenty-two official languages) diverse countries in the world. With roots going back over one thousand years, India's caste system provided a way to manage this diversity. While the system has lost influence in recent decades, it continues to provide social and economic structure to modern Indian society. India won independence from the UK in 1947 following an extended nationalist movement led by Mohandas Gandhi and grounded in civil disobedience. From independence through 1990, India's economy was centrally planned, although the private sector enjoyed space to develop. Since 1991, India has been engaged in an ongoing process of economic restructuring and liberalization. Hindu nationalism is experiencing both social and political resurgence in India today, and relations with Pakistan remain problematic.

Culture

India's history, size, and diversity make it difficult to identify a general culture for the entire country. Indeed, as has been true for most of India's history, Indian culture is in a continuing state of change. India is following the worldwide trend of increased urbanization, materialism, literacy, education, and access to technology and information—all resulting in a heightened awareness of inequalities and expectations about addressing those inequalities. Despite its weakening power, the caste system continues to play an important role in structuring social interactions. Acceptance of one's place in life, including acceptance of the caste system, continues to moderate cultural change throughout India.

Establishing Culture3 Dialogue

Because Indians come from such a varied, rapidly changing culture, building cultural bridges will challenge those working in India or with Indians in other countries. In general, Indians expect somewhat autocratic and charismatic leadership. Develop relaxed expectations about punctuality, acceptance of Indian ambivalence about time, and a mindset that sees delay of social functions as a normal occurrence. Avoid direct confrontation; actions that save face are an important part of developing and maintaining productive relationships. To preserve group unity and save face for Indian colleagues, be cautious about overt assessment and incentive programs focused on individual performance.

Indonesia

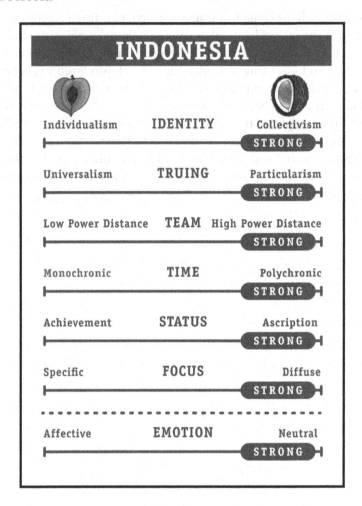

Highlights

Indonesia is strongly polychronic; flexible agendas and time commitments are part of doing business. As in other Coconut cultures, status often comes from one's social affiliations, school connections, kinship group, or home region rather than from personal achievement. Indonesian society is strongly particularist and collectivist, obligating family and group loyalties along with actions that require self-sacrifice for group welfare. Power distance is also high, yet the boss-employee relationship does not stop outside the office door.

History

Indonesia is made up of a 3,200-mile archipelago of volcanic islands between Asia and Australia. It is the home to more Muslims than any other country. Prior to European colonization and conflict over the spice trade in the seventeenth and eighteenth centuries, Indonesia was the center of Hindu and Buddhist kingdoms and then part of an Islamic state. It was colonized under the name Dutch East Indies from 1670 to the early 1900s. Japan occupied Indonesia during World War II. Indonesia achieved formal independence in 1949 and alternated between authoritarian and democratic government until 1999, when democracy was established. In the recent past, Indonesia has enjoyed periods of strong economic growth, particularly under authoritarian leaders who argued that economic stability and development are closely linked with tight control of political freedoms. The Asian financial crisis (1997–1999) hit Indonesia particularly hard, challenging this notion of "guided democracy." Among Indonesia's concerns today are finding ways to address the demands of development while also protecting its vast rain forest, maintaining peace and stability between competing factions inside the country, and addressing pressing problems like the aftermath of the 2004 tsunami (which killed 240,000 people) and the 2009 earthquake that hit the province of West Sumatra.

Culture

Although Indonesia is made up of many different cultures, mainstream Indonesian culture is classically Coconut. The family is the basis of cultural values and loyalties. Commitments to personal relationships often make time commitments more flexible. Society is hierarchically structured. One's place in a particular relationship determines one's duties toward others in that relationship. As a subordinate, for example, one is expected to seek out and demonstrate respect for a superior's opinion and advice, even if that superior is not qualified in the area in question. In an effort to save face, Indonesians avoid embarrassing others at all costs. This aversion includes a reluctance to disagree, particularly in public.

Establishing Culture3 Dialogue

Exercise a great deal of patience. A strong relationship based on mutual trust is essential before specific business activities can be started. This means spending significant amounts of time in socialization activities with those at the top of a company and with those responsible for technical matters before agreeing to a contract. Ask for clarification often. Take the time to understand the concerns and priorities of subordinates, and avoid confrontation; these actions will go a long way in building consensus and support. Incentives for improved performance should focus on group achievement rather than on individual performance. Maintain distance from your subordinates while also demonstrating parental concern for their welfare.

Iran

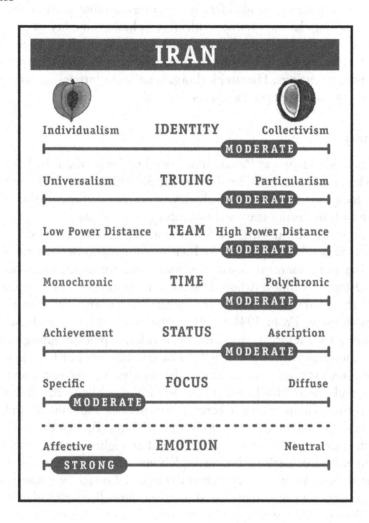

Highlights

Although it has an overall Coconut culture, Iranian society exhibits some Peach characteristics. Iranians are moderately polychronic. Relationships make commitments to a particular time more fluid, and completion of tasks may be interrupted by other tasks of equal importance or by individual needs. Status generally comes from one's social position or age. Iran is a moderately collectivist society with long-term loyalties to family, extended family, and in-group that override societal rules and regulations. Iranian culture emphasizes quality of life and conflict resolution through compromise and negotiation. Emotional expression is an acceptable form of communication, typical in both public and private settings. Hierarchical organization in business is accepted, reflecting power inequalities in society.

History

Anciently known as Persia, Iran is slightly larger than the US state of Alaska and is covered by diverse terrain with a variety of climates. Iran today has the twenty-ninth-largest economy in the world. Islam came to Iran during the seventh century and has played a significant role for much of Iran's history. Starting with the Safavid dynasty in the 1500s, Shia Islam (tightly linked with nationalism) became the state religion and a source of resistance against the continued expansion of the Ottoman Empire (whose leaders were Sunni Muslims). It wasn't until the Pahlavi dynasty of the twentieth century that Iran began to modernize. From 1941 to 1979, the shahs (kings) implemented Western-style reforms, loosened social rules, expanded voting rights, and industrialized the country.[18,19] The abandonment of Islamic principles, however, led to a revolution, the expulsion of the last shah from Iran, and the establishment of an Islamic republic under Ruhollah Khomeini. Khomeini made certain that all laws and cultural and social practices adhered strictly to Islamic dictates. Broken ties with the West, state sponsorship of terrorism, and an eight-year war with Iraq led to economic decline. Following Khomeini's death, Iran has experienced periods of moderate liberalization followed by conservative retreat from reform. Following Mahmoud Ahmadinejad's reelection as president in 2009, widespread protests broke out. Although they were eventually squashed by government forces, protests continue to take place, including demonstrations amidst other uprisings throughout the Middle East in 2011. Today, Iran continues to challenge the West with tactics such as efforts to develop nuclear power, threats to close the Strait of Hormuz (a key shipping route), and the downing of a US spy drone in 2011.

Culture

As in other Coconut cultures, the family is the basis of all social structure and the source of social networks in Iran. Since that structure fosters strong group relationships, everyone is expected to take responsibility for other members of his or her group. The entire family or group experiences a member's shame or loss of face. With a flexible approach to time, Iranians see attention to personal needs and to social-network obligations as more important than punctuality. Although there are small signs of increased tolerance for unorthodox behavior and ideas, Iran maintains a rigid code of belief and behavior in public. The need for security may dampen initiatives for innovation and change.

Establishing Culture3 Dialogue

Iranians prefer to do business with those they know and trust, so plan to take time socializing outside the work setting to build trust and develop working relationships. In Iran, management is the management of groups. Take into account an employee's group affiliations when hiring and making promotion decisions, since those decisions will have impacts beyond the individual employee. Focus on strategies that are sensitive to the Iranian value of "working in order to live." These strategies include building consensus, respecting group solidarity, and incentivizing change with rewards like free time and flexibility. Because Iran is a relatively high-power-distance society, demonstrate centralized power, decisiveness, and benevolent concern for subordinates' quality of life while also remaining open to compromise and negotiation.

Israel

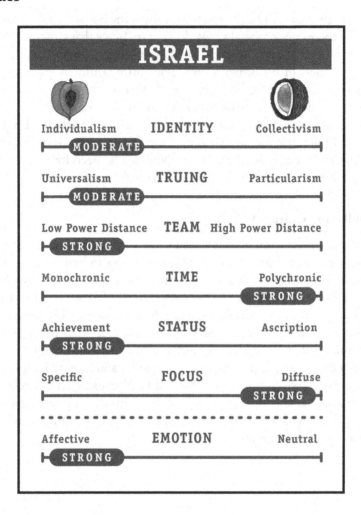

Highlights

Israel has a CocoPeach culture; it does not fall squarely into either the Coconut camp or the Peach camp. Israelis are strongly polychronic, preferring to do several things at once. Because they see themselves as part of one big family, Israelis privilege relationships over strict schedules and business commitments. Israelis also value individual achievement, expecting others to take responsibility for their own actions. While respecting authority, Israelis value open, two-way discussion that leads to pragmatic solutions, even if that discussion means questioning one's superiors. Although universalist values generally structure interaction in Israel, it is a religious state that privileges Jews over other populations, so there is ongoing conflict between universalist and particularist values. Speaking emotionally and using hand gestures and facial expressions for added emphasis are typical parts of communication in Israel. In an effort to address concerns and challenges and quickly move to a solution, Israelis are typically straightforward and even blunt in speaking with others.

History

Sharing borders with Egypt, Jordan, Lebanon, and Syria, Israel occupies approximately eight thousand square miles (making it slightly larger than the US state of New Jersey). Tracing its origins to Abraham, who lived sometime between 2000 and 1501 BCE[20], Israel has since had a history of foreign occupation and intervention. Although Israel formally declared its independence in May 1948, establishing a Jewish homeland and a multiparty parliamentary democracy, it is still impacted by unresolved conflict with the Arab world in general and with the Palestinians in particular. In 2012, the United Nations recognized a Palestinian state that includes the West Bank and the Gaza Strip, but the area remains under Israeli control. With one of the world's top forty export economies, Israel enjoys a high standard of living. A strong university system and a highly educated workforce have fueled a high-tech boom and rapid economic growth.

Culture

Although its people are primarily Jewish (76 percent), Israel also has a significant Muslim population (17 percent) as well as other minorities. Reflecting that diversity, Hebrew and Arabic are Israel's official languages, but English is widely used. Like many Peaches, Israelis enjoy casual, informal, low-power-distance relationships. They value direct communication characterized by honesty and clarity. Israelis' communication style is typically straightforward and assertive, and they prefer to resolve conflict through direct, face-to-face encounters. As Israel moves away from Zionist and collectivistic roots, individualistic values are on the rise. Israelis value individual initiative and achievement. Like many Coconuts, Israelis have a flexible view of time, focusing more on the present than on the future. They prefer to do several things at once instead of spending long stretches of time on one task, and they use valued relationships to prioritize tasks. Israeli culture is diffuse. An Israeli views his or her company as a second family (a mindset enhanced by the smallness of the country) and tends to blur the lines between private and public life.

Establishing Culture3 Dialogue

Plan to spend time outside work getting to know your counterparts and others socially. Having relationships of trust will open up communication and create opportunities for problem solving. To further develop relationships, welcome open discussion and the free sharing of ideas, feelings, and opinions. Blunt or direct speech and passionate debates with lots of interrupting should not be interpreted as aggressive or disrespectful. Being included in such conversations is a sign that you are considered part of "one big family." Bring flexibility to work plans, knowing that work schedules will be changed to accommodate employee initiative, and aim those plans at quickly finding solutions. In one-on-one and small-group interactions, it is appropriate to share feelings openly, speak loudly, and add emphasis with hand gestures.

Italy

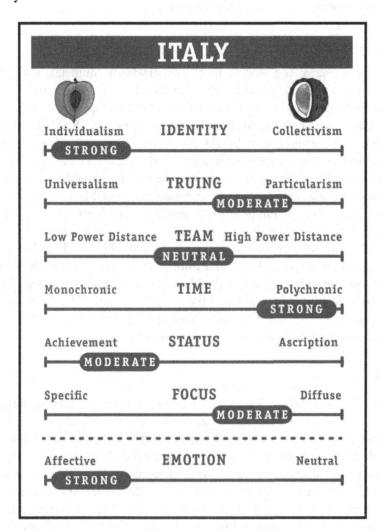

Highlights

Italian culture is CocoPeach, not easily categorized as strictly Peach or Coconut. Italians are strongly polychronic, particularly outside of the major cities and in the southern part of the country. Individual status comes from working hard and achieving. Italians often bend the rules for family, friends, and others in their social networks, but they hold hard to rules for strangers. Emotional communication is key and is expected in both private and business relationships.

History

Italy is one of the world's most-industrialized countries, with the eighth-largest economy on Earth. Historically, Italy was central to the Roman Empire and a key contributor to the development of Western civilization and culture. Modern Italy was unified in 1870, and its experience before and during World War II was characterized by fascism, dictatorial rule under Benito Mussolini. Italy became a republic in 1946. Ever since, it has remained a fractious democratic republic, struggling through scandal and corruption. Although designed to prevent totalitarianism, Italy's current political system (based on loose and frequently changing coalitions) weakens government stability; there have been more than fifty-seven successive governments since World War II. Today, Italy struggles to address challenges like immigration, corruption, high unemployment, organized crime, and wide economic disparities, particularly between the successful north and the struggling south. The 2008 global financial crisis and the ongoing economic crisis in Europe continue to plague Italian efforts to put its house in order.

Culture

While most Italians identify themselves as Roman Catholic, Italian society is largely secular. Social interaction is a critical part of daily life, making time commitments more flexible and less urgent. The economic divide between northern Italy and southern Italy is reflected in the regions' contrasting approaches to time. In northern Italy (Peach), time is viewed as a resource not to be wasted; punctuality, reliability, and organization all go together in determining economic success. In southern Italy (Coconut), people approach time in a much more leisurely, nonlinear way. Social connection and agreeableness, not individual assertiveness, often drive individual action.

Establishing Culture3 Dialogue

Emphasize and reaffirm the importance of personal relationships as the starting point for doing business. Dressing appropriately, showing enthusiasm, and taking time to get to know counterparts are all important parts of that relationship-building process. Expect Italians to be emotional and demonstrative, using a variety of hand and facial expressions to add emphasis to discussion. Negotiations and group discussions are free-flowing, with expectations that everyone will have a say but that final decisions may not be reached. Thus, meetings often do not closely follow agendas. Heated conversation and arguments are fairly typical and do not necessarily mean that a discussion is going badly. Interrupting a speaker or presenter is acceptable.

Japan

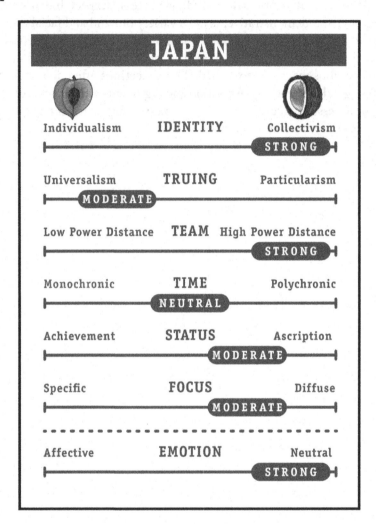

Highlights

Except for some universalist values, Japan tends toward Coconut culture. Japan is a highly structured and collectivist society. Clear social rules and duties based on one's position or status dictate behavior in most situations. Although mindsets are changing somewhat, status is based on one's background, the ranking of the school one graduated from, and other associations. The welfare of the group is of supreme importance. Group members are expected to contribute to group harmony by acting within the prevailing social structure and performing the duties of respect dictated by their positions. In other words, individuals are expected to conform to group norms and to sacrifice individual advantage for the good of the group. Leaders maintain high power distance in their management of subordinates, minimizing casual or informal interaction. In Japan, to show one's emotions (particularly in public) is to lose face.

History

Consisting of four major islands surrounded by hundreds of small ones, Japan (nicknamed the Land of the Rising Sun) has taken vastly different approaches toward the rest of the world throughout its history. US Admiral Matthew Perry forcibly opened Japan to international trade in 1853, leading to the end of the Tokugawa shogunate (1603–1868) and its strict enforcement of social order and isolationism. Japan emerged as a regional power through war, defeating China in 1895 and Russia in 1905. Japan industrialized quickly and pursued regional dominance in World War II by invading China and bombing the US naval base at Pearl Harbor, Hawaii—and sealing its own fate by leading the US to finally join the war. Emerging from defeat, Japan renounced war, instituted democratic reforms, and aggressively pursued rapid modernization. Although it has been experiencing economic stagnation since the 1990s and struggling with the aftermath of crises like the March 2011 earthquake and tsunami, Japan remains an economic powerhouse, with an economy in the top five world-wide.

Culture

From the legacy of the shoguns, Japan remains a stratified society with formal rules of interaction and regular use of titles. Japanese society is also collectivist; loyalty to one's groups is seen as essential to maintaining harmony. Working long hours for one's employer, for example, is seen as a duty to the company. Japanese people generally honor age and tradition and show deference and respect toward superiors. Although younger generations may challenge cultural norms, conformity in appearance continues to be important. Politeness and saving face often mean that Japanese people avoid saying "no" directly. "Yes" may simply mean "I understand" rather than agreement. Saving face also dictates that divisive topics be avoided.

Establishing Culture3 Dialogue

Keep group harmony and expectations of a long-term relationship as high priorities. Achieving these objectives will require dressing and acting the part. Developing connections with Japanese counterparts who can provide introductions will go far in building rapport in new situations. Efforts to change subordinates' behavior, particularly in ways that may cause an employee to lose face, are typically unsuccessful and damaging to relationships. To succeed more often in negotiations, respect the importance of group decision-making and consensus. This may mean that negotiations between two individuals may not lead to a specific agreement, since the Japanese negotiator may need to consult with the group he or she represents. Absence of emotion on the part of Japanese people does not mean lack of interest.

Malaysia

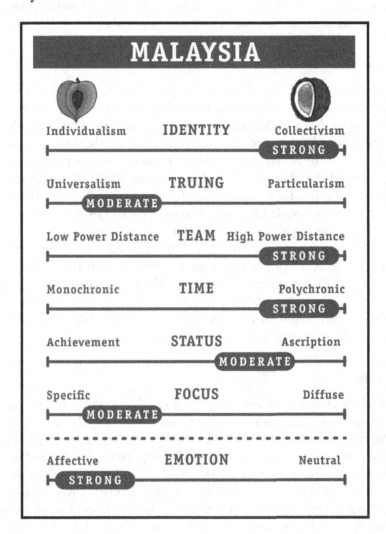

Highlights

Malaysia has a Coconut culture, and its people are strongly poly-chronic. Deadlines are flexible and projects don't follow linear plans, since one cannot anticipate forces beyond individual control that will alter those plans. Malaysians' efforts focus strongly on group welfare rather than on individual gain. As in the patriarchally organized Malaysian family, leaders are expected to maintain high power distance in dealing with subordinates. Malaysians are strongly affective. Showing emotion in business negotiations is acceptable and appropriate.

History

Malaysia is made up of thirteen states.[21,22] Its recorded history begins in the fourteenth century. Following Portuguese capture of the port city Malacca in the early sixteenth century, the Dutch and later the British took control of the city. By the early 1900s, the British controlled all of the Malay states, making them colonies or protectorates. Japan invaded and occupied Malaysia during World II, heightening Malaysian desire for independence from foreign influence. In 1957, the UK granted Malaysia independence. Sparked by economic inequities and privileged access for the Chinese population of Malaysia, racial tension broke into rioting in 1969. Subsequent programs were relatively successful in bringing about constitutional reform and the removal of wide economic disparities. Malaysia enjoyed strong economic growth in the 1990s. Still, civil unrest, ethnic tensions and violence, and heightened worries about terrorist threats continue to plague Malaysia today.

Culture

Malaysia is a multiethnic society, with Malays making up the largest group but with significant Chinese and Indian populations as well. Like other Coconut cultures, Malaysian culture emphasizes the welfare of the group over that of the individual. Cooperation, loyalty, and unity are cohesive values for both families and Malaysian society in general. Ethnic identity often overshadows national identity. Promoting harmonious group relations includes saving face and avoiding shaming, insulting, or putting someone on the spot. Islam, Malaysia's official religion, provides another source of group identity. Individual status (granted by wealth, position, education, etc.), however, challenges the importance of the group. Malaysians see success, failure, opportunity, and misfortune as forces beyond individual control; such events are believed to be the result of fate or God's will.

Establishing Culture3 Dialogue

Respect the importance of group consensus. Spend initial meetings building rapport, delaying in-depth business discussions for later meetings. Show appropriate respect for authority figures and avoid public confrontation, even when the goal is to promote change in Malaysian subordinates' individual behavior. Play the part of a leader, acting in ways dictated by high power distance. In an effort to not cause others to lose face, Malaysians often avoid saying no. To achieve clarity, check a response by phrasing yes-no questions in different ways.

Mexico

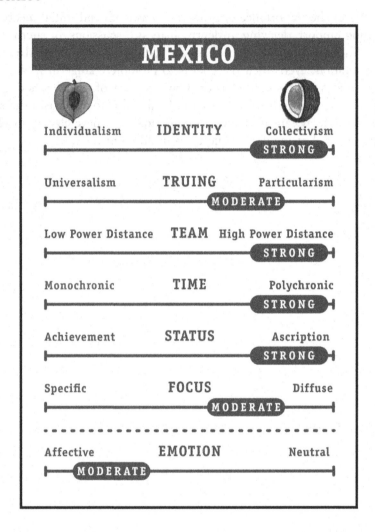

Highlights

In Mexico—which has a Coconut culture—there is little sense of urgency regarding time. Punctuality and long-term planning are not high priorities; developing, maintaining, and improving networks and relationships may take precedence over the bottom line. Within an organization, status determines responsibilities and puts responsibility on the person to help the organization accomplish its goals. Employees accept and are responsive to high power distance from leaders. It is expected that those within an organization will sacrifice individual priorities and needs to meet the needs of the group. Achievement is more about group performance than about individual success.

History

Spanish conquest, colonialism, and the imposition of Roman Catholicism left Mexicans with a tradition of authoritarianism and paternalism. For centuries, the Catholic Church controlled religious, social, and political leadership; property; and capital. With time, land ownership was expanded but remained limited to a few powerful priests and members of religious orders. Amidst wildly unequal distributions of economic power, most interactions were governed by patterns of control and reciprocal obligations between *mestizos* (people of mixed indigenous and Spanish backgrounds) and political or religious leaders. Following independence in the early nineteenth century, Mexican *caudillos*, or regional governors, built on these traditions of patriarchal leadership, providing protection for loyal followers. This was a time, however, of turmoil and political instability across the country. It was not until the early twentieth century that the Institutional Revolutionary Party (PRI) was formed, providing an enduring structure to support a national government.[23] By accommodating the interests of and distributing power to leaders of the major sectors of society, the PRI was central to consolidating state institutions and providing social stability. Since the 1990s, Mexico has struggled to address authoritarian leadership structures, inefficient and corrupt bureaucracy, drug-cartel-related violence, resource distribution, and public criticism of leadership.

Culture

As in other Coconut cultures, Mexican family structure provides insight into social hierarchy and appropriate relationships. Paternalism and autocratic leadership coupled with high power distance (embodied in the *caudillos*) is viewed as the norm, leading to hierarchical organizational structures. Despite this style, there is little sense of urgency in the use of time, and little effort may be spent in long-term planning. While showing loyalty to the organization and fulfilling obligations to supervisors and others are important, personal relationships with family and friends trump those obligations. It is often through networks of friendships and personal acquaintances that individuals define and pursue their own self-interest. When facing both hard times and opportunities, Mexicans draw upon the reciprocal obligations built up through this interpersonal strategy. Decisions may be based more on whom one knows and trusts and less on merit or rationality.

Establishing Culture3 Dialogue

Work within the high-power-distance structure prevalent in Mexico. Be charismatic, assertive, and tough while also maintaining cordial interpersonal relations. Develop project plans that include time for employee interaction. Mexican employees may see little use in company policies and procedures, even those that directly affect them. On the other hand, strategies for change may be more accepted if they are grounded in the welfare of the entire group.

Norway

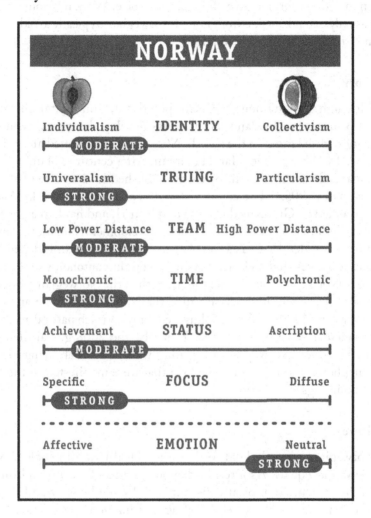

Highlights

Although Norway has a strong Peach culture, Norwegians emphasize the importance of relationships and quality of life. Even more than its Scandinavian neighbors, Norway is strongly monochronic. Norwegians are proud of their tolerance toward others, viewing adherence to universal rules of behavior as a key component of Norwegian society. Although individualism and individual accomplishment are important, organizational structure is typically flat. The decision-making process often includes efforts to give all involved a voice. Work relationships do not usually extend outside work hours. Norwegians typically avoid strong demonstrations of emotion in public.

History

Although mountainous, sparsely populated, and containing only about 3 percent arable land, Norway has developed a strong economy (twenty-eighth largest in the world). Norway was first united around the year 872 by Viking leader Harald Fairhair. After centuries of union with Denmark, Sweden, or both, Norway established its own constitutional monarchy in 1905.[24] The country stayed neutral during World War I, was occupied by Germany during World War II, and has had a postwar period of political stability and economic development. Norway balances its European identity (it is a member of NATO) with an independent streak (it has resisted EU membership), retaining autonomy and confidence in Norway's resources and the strength of the Norwegian economy. A Norwegian committee has awarded the Nobel Peace Prize annually since the early 1900s.[25] With a robust economy and rich natural-resource endowments, Norway was little affected by the 2008 global financial crisis. However, Norway is still dealing with the destabilizing effects of xenophobia and radical nationalism that were manifested in the July 2011 bombings and shootings.

Culture

Norwegians strongly hold to the Peach ideal that all people should be viewed as equals. As a result, demonstrations of wealth and financial achievement are typically discouraged. While honesty and sincerity are important traits when building and maintaining relationships, Norwegians are transactional and do not require a long-standing relationship with a person or organization to do business. At the same time, they prefer to do business with those who demonstrate trustworthiness. Norwegians are direct communicators and appreciate those who are confident and straightforward, even when expressing disagreement. Women are highly respected in the workplace and receive equal pay for equal work.

Establishing Culture3 Dialogue

Demonstrate respect for organizational and decision-making norms. With flat organizational structures that encourage consultation with the group before making choices, be sure to budget sufficient time to arrive at final decisions. Providing a detailed meeting agenda in advance, presenting precise and concrete proposals during meetings, and staying focused on the business at hand will also send a message of competence. Promote change by focusing on transformational leadership and feminine cultural values. Demonstrate modest, competent leadership and build consensus to develop a new vision and to gather support for change from key stakeholders. Employees and colleagues will respond positively to a vision that is built on past accomplishments and identifies future opportunities.

Poland

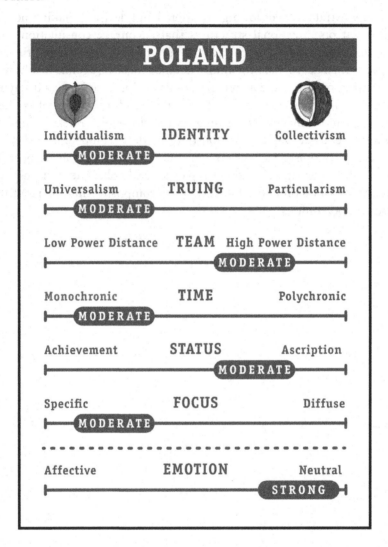

Highlights

Polish culture is CocoPeach; it does not fit neatly into either the Peach or the Coconut mold. It is moderately monochronic. Time, punctuality, and deadlines all organize and structure life. Poles emphasize individual performance rather than the welfare of the group when pursuing change and progress. Leaders maintain moderately high power distance. Poles typically communicate little emotion, particularly in superior-subordinate conversations and when interacting with strangers.

History

Given its flat terrain and its location at the heart of central Europe, Poland has been vulnerable to territory-seeking armies for much of its history. Its borders have changed multiple times. A major power in Europe during the late Middle Ages, Poland wrote the second constitution in the world in 1791, giving its serfs state protection. Prussia, Austria, and Russia invaded and partitioned Poland in 1795. It became an independent nation again at the end of World War I. Invaded by Germany and Russia during World War II, Poland was divided once more, then unified under a communist government in 1947. Although labor-union strikes were crushed in 1981, changes in Poland and in the Soviet Union brought about democratic government. Subsequent "shock therapy" failed to produce the economic growth expected; corruption, high unemployment, and an uncompetitive agricultural system stood in the way. Since then, the pace of economic reform has slowed as Poland pursues greater global integration. Now among the thirty largest economies in the world, Poland joined NATO in 1999 and the EU in 2004.

Culture

Like Peaches, Poles value individualism and see practicality and self-reliance as important qualities. They are outspoken and generous but adhere to formal rules of interaction. As in Coconut cultures, the family is the most important Polish group, forming the basis of one's social and business network. Extending and returning favors are important parts of maintaining this network and getting things done, particularly when cutting through bureaucracy. With 90 percent of Poland's citizens belonging to the Roman Catholic Church, the Church has a significant impact on social values and serves as a model of patriarchal leadership.

Establishing Culture3 Dialogue

Let your Polish counterparts set the appropriate level of formality. Take the time to build relationships by getting to know your Polish colleagues before getting down to business. This practice will often mean investing time in informal activities like lunches and dinners. Negotiations are often inconclusive, as Polish negotiators will need to check any tentative agreements with superiors before final decisions are made. Promote change by incentivizing individual performance.

Russia

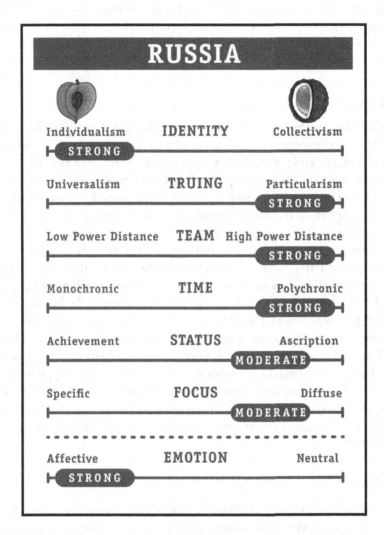

Highlights

As a Coconut culture, Russian society has strong polychronic values; time is not seen as urgent. In delivering services, businesses are not bound by hard-and-fast deadlines. When plans are made, they are apt to change, reflecting changing priorities, shifting commitments, and other unknown factors. Russians' aggressive pursuit of individual self-interest, combined with a relative sense of morality that is informed by relationship networks, further contributes to changeable rules of operation. High power distance remains strong, with corresponding respect for authority figures and their privileges. Strong public display of emotion is common and acceptable.

History

Covering nine time zones, Russia is the largest country in the world. Its historical experience has been one of ironfisted leadership and economic, social, and political upheaval. Although the 1917 Bolshevik revolution was a rejection of imperial Russia, the model of a strong leader (embodied by rulers like Peter the Great) and a centralized state has been a unifying thread in Russia's twentieth-century experience. Decades of totalitarian rule meant that most Russians focused on survival through demonstrating political loyalty and conforming to standards set by the Communist Party. When Mikhail Gorbachev initiated drastic political and economic reforms in the mid-1980s, increased freedom and contact with the West ultimately resulted in the dissolution of the Soviet Union in 1991. While Russia initially experienced euphoria over the movement toward democracy and market capitalism, post-Soviet leaders like Boris Yeltsin and Vladimir Putin still gravitated toward the historical model of strong, authoritarian leadership; elite privilege; and suppression of dissent. The end of communism in Russia has meant greater freedom to participate in creating one's own destiny, but it has also made life more uncertain, as Russian society continues to go through a period of transition.

Culture

Russia holds mostly Coconut values. These preferences come from its experiences with traditional society prior to communism; totalitarianism during most of the twentieth century; and social, economic, and political upheaval in the 1990s. Russians retain a strong group mentality, meaning they are sometimes more risk averse when it comes to individual initiative. This mentality also means that Russians will loyally continue working at a job even when they have not been paid for months. Yet within that context of conformity, Russians feel little social responsibility and will pursue highly individualistic ends, challenging Western norms of ethical behavior. Russian society remains stratified, with high power distance mandating respect for authority and the privileges that come with power. Getting ahead in Russia often means ignoring moral standards and rules instead of improving performance. Because of social and economic instability, Russians often pursue short-term gains rather than making long-term plans.

Establishing Culture3 Dialogue

Find ways to encourage and facilitate cultural synergies. Understand both Russia's historical experience and the cultural realities in which business is conducted today. Provide clear vision and administrative competency. Build relationships based on mutual respect and motivated by self-interest when working with Russian leadership teams. Expectations about rapid change and meeting specific performance objectives must be tempered by the realities of a polychronic society.

Saudi Arabia

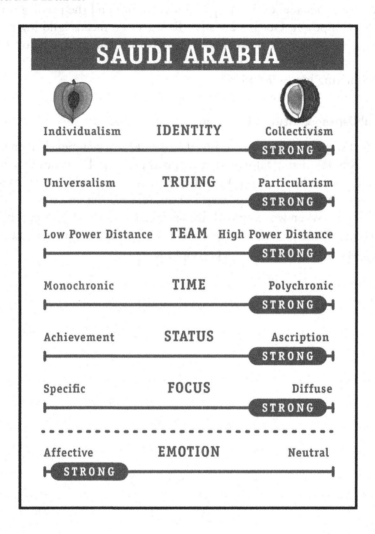

Highlights

As in other Coconut cultures, for Saudis, the clock is much more forgiving of the inevitable delays that are part of daily life. Relationships are more important than tasks; schedules and agendas are flexible and are adjusted to address unforeseen relationship obligations. Power, title, and position are critical in Saudi Arabia. While Islamic values are seen as universal, particularistic relationships provide obligations and privileges through group membership. Saudis see group loyalty and welfare as more important than the pursuit of individual recognition. Society is organized hierarchically, with patriarchy and high power distance viewed as normal parts of superior-subordinate relationships. Emotional expression is a typical part of communication.

History

Saudi Arabia dominates the Arabian Peninsula both in geographic size and in economic significance. The birth and development of Islam dramatically impacted civilization in the area. Under Islam, warring tribes on the Arabian Peninsula were united, social practices changed, and a Muslim empire expanded to Asia, northern Africa, and other regions, bringing advancements in astronomy, medicine, and mathematics to those areas. The empire began to decline in the thirteenth century, leading to ongoing skirmishes between rival nomadic tribes across the Arabian Peninsula. Taking advantage of Islam as a potential unifying factor for the peninsula, Abdul Aziz ibn Saud leveraged his position as a tribal leader and the head of the Wahhabi religious order to be declared king of Saudi Arabia in 1932. His family has dominated the monarchy since that time. Thanks to strong growth in the energy sector, Saudi Arabia is one of the twenty-five largest economies in the world today. Saudi Arabia is home to Islam's two most sacred sites: Mecca and Medina. Although Saudi Arabia hosted an international coalition to repel Iraq's 1990 invasion of Kuwait and has moved toward political liberalization, it retains many of its conservative customs. Today, Saudi Arabia is harnessing its natural-resource endowments (it has 18 percent of global oil reserves) to build a modern public infrastructure, invest in education, and silence militant voices within society.

Culture

In the solidly Coconut Saudi culture, the family and Islam are the central organizers of society. Showing respect for patriarchs, political and business leaders, and religious officials is essential to good relationships. Saudis are generally relaxed about time. Because they prefer to work with those they know and trust, they spend a great deal of time making and enhancing connections and relationships, particularly in informal settings. Building and tapping into connections to Saudi social groups often opens doors for business opportunities. Saudis tend to avoid acknowledging their own inabilities, and they lose respect for others who readily admit theirs.

Establishing Culture3 Dialogue

Spend a great deal of time in getting-to-know-you activities, followed by continued demonstrations of personal connection, with your Saudi counterparts and their families. It is challenging to promote increased efficiency and productive activity among Saudi subordinates. Adhere to classic bureaucratic behavior, spending more time in symbolic and ceremonial events than in supervising work or in making decisions about resource allocation.

South Africa

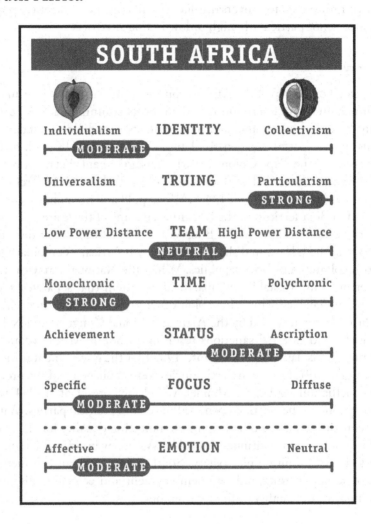

Highlights

South Africa's multicultural, multilinguistic society is CocoPeach, difficult to classify as strictly Peach or Coconut; different groups align differently along many of the cultural dimensions. Despite those differences, South African businesspeople are typically strongly monochronic. Status derives in part from one's ethnic identity, educational and institutional affiliations, and political-party membership. South Africans are strongly particularistic, privileging family and organizational affiliations over commitments to universal values. Unlike in most societies, power distance is not particularly high or low in South Africa.

History

Located on the tip of the African continent, South Africa is primarily savannah and semidesert and is known for its stunning natural beauty. Early French, Dutch, and German colonists called Boers established farms in the coastal areas in the late 1600s, and the UK took formal possession of the Cape Colony in 1814. Disagreements between British rulers and the Boers led to Boer migration, called the Great Trek, into the interior in the 1830s and 1840s. When gold and diamonds were discovered in Boer territories, the UK annexed some of those areas, leading to tension and eventually the Boer War (1899–1902). After defeating the Boers, the UK created the Union of South Africa, a combination of British colonies and Boer republics. When the National Party came to power in 1948, it established apartheid, a system that separated racial groups and enabled whites to exploit other groups. Despite internal resistance to apartheid, led by the African National Congress and Nelson Mandela, and external sanctions resulting in South Africa's economic and political isolation, it wasn't until 1989 that the government initiated reform. By 1991, most apartheid policies were abolished and the process of reconciliation was begun. Mandela was elected president in 1994, with participation in the election open to all races and political parties. With a new constitution and a bill of rights guaranteeing equality for all, South African democracy continues to evolve. With eleven official languages and a diverse, multiethnic society, South Africa struggles to increase economic opportunity, reduce unemployment and economic disparity, and improve the quality of life for everyone.

Culture

Despite the end of apartheid, the election of a truly democratic government, and a new constitution protecting the rights of all citizens, South Africa still struggles with its legacy of racial segregation. Getting ahead in South Africa is still connected to relationships and inside knowledge of and access to information and resources. At the same time, individual achievement in sports and other areas of life is strongly emphasized; self-worth is often connected to personal accomplishment. South Africans take pride in the progress they have made in moving away from a racially divided past toward a society that protects and cares for all.

Establishing Culture3 Dialogue

Provide strong direction informed by democratic and participative relationships with subordinates. Be an agent of change who is sensitive to your followers' ideas and needs and also provides pragmatic and creative solutions to problems. Be decisive, but extensive consultation with subordinates and others should precede a final decision. While a task-oriented approach that emphasizes individual performance can be successful, it must be accompanied by actions that demonstrate concern for the whole group.

South Korea

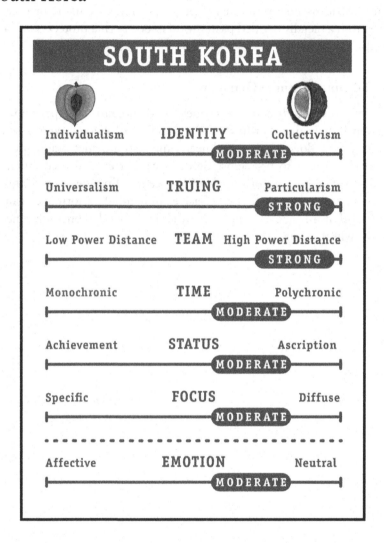

Highlights

South Korea exhibits primarily Coconut characteristics. Factors like age, gender, the university one graduated from, and family background are all powerful determinants of status. Close relationships affect behavior much more than rules do, meaning that South Koreans often bend rules to help a friend, former classmate, or family member. Businesses often motivate their employees by appealing to commitments to group welfare rather than by highlighting individual advantages. Teams are vertically organized, with high power distance between leaders and subordinates. South Koreans typically show little emotion in public, preferring to present themselves as rational.

History

Most outsiders think of Korea as two countries—North and South— but for most of its five-thousand-year history, it has been one nation. Korea is known traditionally as the Land of the Morning Calm. In 1392, the Joseon dynasty was established, surviving until 1910, when Japan annexed Korea. Early in the Joseon dynasty, Confucianism was made Korea's official religion (although it is a philosophy more than a religion today). Korean patriotism is partly rooted in developments such as the Korean script and the world's first movable-type press. After Japan's defeat in World War II, the Soviet Union took temporary control in northern Korea while the US did the same in southern Korea. Disagreements over the form of a new government exploded into the Korean War. Neither side was able to get the upper hand, resulting in a stalemate and a divided Korea that still exist today.[26] Despite tensions along the border—the most heavily armed in the world—South Korea grew rapidly under authoritarian, state-led economic policies, especially during the 1980s. Invoking images of resistance to oppression during the Japanese occupation, students and then others joined in protests, leading to the establishment of democracy in 1987. Today, South Korea ranks among the top fifteen economies in the world.

Culture

South Korean society is a highly structured hierarchy. Language is used to convey honor to superiors and familiarity to equals and subordinates. Because society is vertically ordered (a legacy of Confucianism), all interaction is structured by one's place in a social group or one's status in a relationship. Gender, education, family background, wealth, occupation, school class, and other factors are all important in determining appropriate behavior and expected levels of respect. Social contacts and connections play an important role in business and political success. South Koreans are typically modest when speaking of themselves. They promote group harmony and demonstrate loyalty to the group by using indirect expressions of criticism and other forms of saving face, such as not shaming someone in public.

Establishing Culture3 Dialogue

Put the development of personal relationships before business. These relationships are best developed through connections. Providing information about your status (work title, age, alma mater, etc.) helps South Koreans properly place you into the existing social hierarchy. Exchanging business cards at a first meeting is an important part of this process. In interactions with superiors, colleagues, and subordinates, avoid informality and respect high-power-distance structures. Expect to spend a significant amount of time getting to know your South Korean counterparts before getting down to business. Gift giving and eating out together are expected and serve as relationship builders. In an effort to avoid causing someone to lose face, Koreans typically avoid saying "no." In the same vein, avoid public actions that cause Koreans to lose face.

Spain

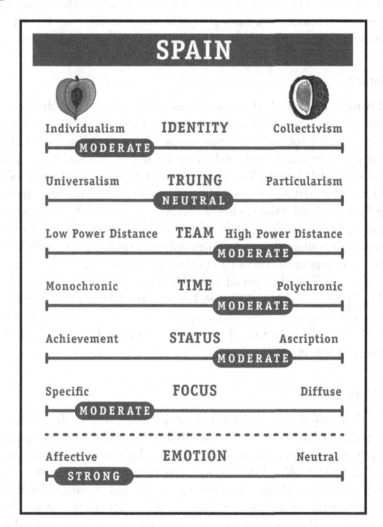

Highlights

Spaniards lean toward Coconut culture in their values and behavior. They tend to be relaxed about planning and deadlines. Punctuality may be justifiably compromised to fulfill relationship commitments. Emphasis is placed on individual merit and performance, and some value is seen in planning for the future through collectivist government programs. Power distance remains high, as demonstrated by the continued use of polite language forms and formal expressions when addressing superiors and customers. Strong expressions of emotion are typical and expected, both in friendships and in business and negotiation settings.

History

Historically controlled by the Roman Empire, the Visigoths, and the Moors, Spain was united in 1469. As one of the world's most powerful empires during the sixteenth century, Spain colonized vast areas of the Americas, extracting much of their wealth to pay Spanish debts. Spain's empire later fell into decline, losing territory throughout the eighteenth century. The first Spanish republic (formed in 1931) was cut short by the Spanish Civil War (1936–1939). For approximately the next four decades, Francisco Franco ruled Spain, exercising censorship, banning divorce, controlling public meetings, suppressing dissidents and liberals, and banning political parties and free-trade unions. Following Franco's death in 1975, Spain formed a parliamentary monarchy that endures today. Spain joined NATO in 1981, joined the EU in 1986, hosted the Summer Olympics in 1992, and adopted the euro as its currency in 2002. Spain's economy is in the top-twenty on Earth and leads the world in wine and olive-oil production.

Culture

Spain's population is highly homogeneous. Over 80 percent of Spaniards consider themselves Catholic, but secular values prevail. It is typical in Spain to focus on relationships and be relaxed about rules and punctuality. Informal social interaction is an important ritual for developing working relationships and in maintaining friendships. Uncomfortable with silence, Spaniards can be demonstrative and boisterous, particularly with friends. Showing emotion is acceptable. While gender inequities have leveled in recent years, Spain still maintains a tradition of male leadership.

Establishing Culture3 Dialogue

Outsiders—particularly Peaches—need to balance their behavior between reserved interaction and more-open displays of emotion. Patience and active participation in social and business rituals will go far in alleviating Spaniards' concerns about the risks of change. Approach conflict and disagreement in a strong and confident yet conciliatory way to make long-lasting connections and find solutions that are acceptable to all parties. Spaniards are not typically concerned about specific planning for every possible contingency, preferring to have the right people in the right places with the proper training and then to rely on those people to take appropriate initiative. Provide inspiration, appropriately encourage initiative, model integrity, and provide space for achievement, and you will find Spanish employees to be responsive.

Sweden

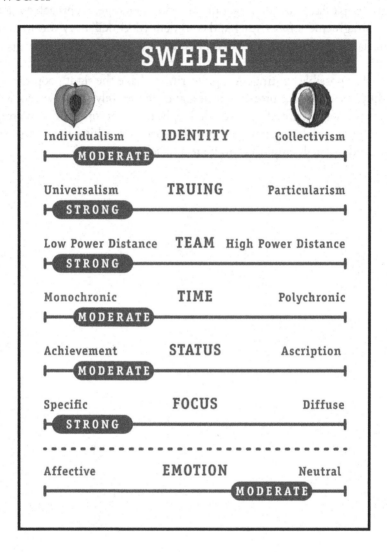

Highlights

Sweden is a Peach culture. Reflecting Swedish society's valuing of equality, flat organizational structure is common. Collaboration that taps into team-member strengths is encouraged. Sweden is committed to equal access to information, resources, and opportunity. Swedes maintain a strong division between work life and private life. While friendships may thrive at work, interaction outside of work is not expected. Strong public expressions of emotion are not common.

History

Situated between Finland and Norway, Sweden has a prosperous economy (one of the top twenty-five largest in the world). Sweden achieved independence in 1523 but did not industrialize until the late nineteenth century. Following World War II, Sweden emerged as one of Europe's leading industrial nations, relying heavily on the international market to compensate for its relatively small domestic market. Sweden developed a peaceful, egalitarian society through the influence of strong social movements (labor, universal suffrage, and women's rights) that accompanied industrialization, ultimately resulting in a parliamentary government and a welfare state grounded in values of equality, social responsibility, and consensus. Sweden today continues to expand its public sector to facilitate moves toward a service-oriented and knowledge-intensive economy and society that are fully integrated into the world economy.

Culture

Central to Swedish culture is a unique combination of egalitarian social values and individualism. On the one hand, the public sphere is structured in ways that value and reward group performance over individual performance. Power distance is rather low, and structures that support decision-making through consensus are well developed. The robust public sector provides many structures, rules, and institutional supports to reduce uncertainty. Swedes have a strong future orientation. With a homogenous society, they are straightforward and interact in predictable ways regardless of context. On the other hand, Swedes place high value on individualism in their private lives. They rarely socialize with fellow workers outside of work and place high value on structures that guarantee noninterference in their private lives.

Establishing Culture3 Dialogue

Learn to work well within a structure that values flat organization. Provide vision, inspiration, and decisive leadership, but strategic direction must be informed by consensus that comes out of efforts to build a collaborative team. Rather than focusing on formality, leading secretive discussions, emphasizing differences, or encouraging competition within a group, focus on sharing knowledge and building a group identity around a common cause.

Switzerland

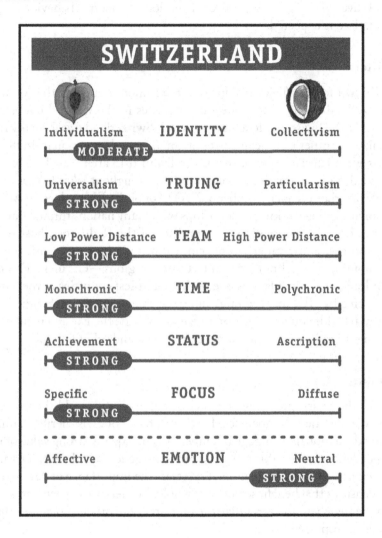

Highlights

The Swiss exhibit strong Peach characteristics. They are strongly monochronic, making punctuality and respect for timelines essential. Status is tightly connected to education, effective performance of one's responsibilities, and success in the business world. The Swiss take pride in their sense of tolerance and value low power distance in the workplace.

They are also strongly specific, making a sharp separation between their work lives and their private lives. Emotionally neutral behavior in the workplace is expected.

History

Known for the majestic Alps that cover more than half the country, Switzerland is one of the oldest democracies in the world. First established as the Swiss Confederation in 1291, Switzerland was formally recognized by other European powers as an independent nation in 1648.[27,28] Switzerland declared permanent neutrality in 1815 after Napoleon briefly invaded, and it maintained that neutrality throughout World Wars I and II. Switzerland is not a member of NATO or of the EU. It does, however, maintain strong working relationships with many nations throughout the world, host the International Committee of the Red Cross, host some UN offices, and regularly broker peace negotiations and conferences. Combining three linguistic and cultural regions—German, French, and Italian—Switzerland is one of the wealthiest countries in the world measured by GDP per capita. Among the challenges facing Switzerland today are addressing its decision to remain outside the EU and regulating immigration in ways that maintain its high standard of living.

Culture

For the Swiss, promptness and close adherence to established schedules demonstrates competence. Partly as a result of Swiss heritage, unity around a national self-image is tempered by an equally strong value of independence from conformity. The Swiss are generally tolerant, see value in democratic decision-making, and stress the importance of developing consensuses that benefit society as a whole. Leaders are expected to serve "in the trenches" and recognize the importance of others, no matter their levels of responsibility.

Establishing Culture3 Dialogue

Work within a value structure that recognizes the benefits of hierarchy but also emphasizes building close links with subordinates. Developing those links requires transformational leadership: draw on pragmatic solutions arrived at through consensus, inspire subordinates to improve performance, and demonstrate decisiveness when necessary. Be self-sacrificing and modest, showing willingness to work as long and as hard as your employees. To develop cooperative teams, integrate team members into decision-making processes in ways that show respect for the team members' needs and expectations.

Taiwan

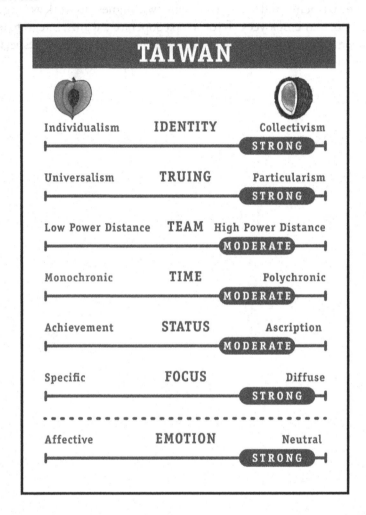

Highlights

Taiwan has a Coconut culture, including a collectivist society in which status comes from one's group memberships. As in China, Confucian values provide structure and protocols for business practices as well as public and private interactions. Taiwanese people are most comfortable working with members of their family, school, and other networks. Efforts to maintain and honor those relationships are seen as valuable and essential. Loyalty to in-group networks often trumps societal rules and regulations. Taiwanese organizational structure reflects the values of high power distance and hierarchy. Both employers and employees have specific responsibilities of respect that extend beyond the workplace. Taiwanese people are reserved, avoiding demonstrations of emotion.

History

Located approximately one hundred miles off the east coast of China, Taiwan's economy is among the top twenty-five economies in the world. Taiwan became a province of China under the Manchus in 1683. Following Chinese defeat in the Sino-Japanese War, Taiwan was ceded to Japan in 1895 and remained under Japanese control until the end of World War II. Taiwan achieved new strategic significance when Chiang Kai-shek's Nationalist troops fled there to escape Mao Zedong's growing communist army in mainland China. When return to mainland China became impossible, Chiang established the Republic of China (ROC) in Taiwan, claiming his organization to be the only legitimate government for all of China. Taiwan lost recognition as a sovereign country when mainland China (the People's Republic of China, or PRC) was admitted to the United Nations. However, Taiwan retains strong diplomatic relations with the US. Initially an authoritarian, one-party state, Taiwan enjoyed strong economic growth, modernization, and development, particularly in the 1980s. Following the lifting of martial law in 1987, Taiwan implemented democratic reform. Although affected by the Asian financial crisis (1997–1999), Taiwan continues to grow economically. Economic ties to the PRC continue to deepen. After sixty years of tense relations, the PRC and Taiwan initiated direct talks in 2009.

Culture

Guanxi (关系) (see chapter 4) is central to social interaction. Obeying superiors, showing decorum, and avoiding embarrassing someone publicly are all ways to maintain *guanxi*. Everyone is expected to demonstrate appropriate respect for the hierarchical social relationships that structure Taiwanese society. Taiwanese people avoid public displays of emotion. Publicly challenging an authority figure is also avoided. Loyalty to the group, pride in the nation and its economic progress, hard work, and a reserved temperament are all components of Taiwanese character.

Establishing Culture3 Dialogue

Start by developing *guanxi* with your Taiwanese counterparts. Trust can be built by spending time outside the office in social situations and by demonstrating appropriate respect for those holding positions of power. When leading and negotiating, protect others from losing face. Bring vision and provide "orders" for carrying out that vision, but successful implementation will hinge on the strength of *guanxi* already in place. Efforts to change individual behavior may be perceived as public confrontations, while messages of collective responsibility are more likely to result in desired changes in behavior.

Turkey

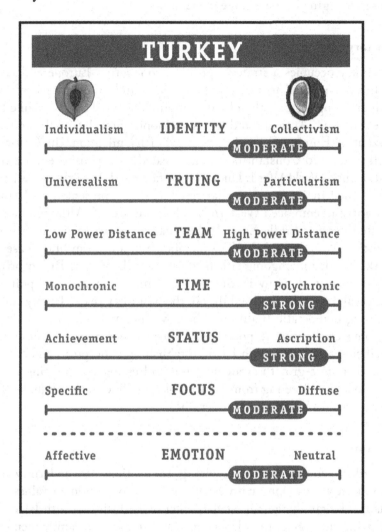

Highlights

As in other Coconut cultures, for Turks, relationship duties and similar commitments are more important than strict adherence to timetables, schedules, and appointments. Titles, seniority, and age are clear signals of status. Rules are less important than loyalty to one's family and social circles. Group membership and the collective are often the starting point when doing business. Power distance remains moderately high, although this is changing in the younger generation.

History

Turkey occupies a strategic position connecting Europe and Asia. It has been home to many notable cities and civilizations over its rich and long history: the Hittite Empire; ancient Troy; Roman cities like Ephesus, Antioch, and Constantinople (now Istanbul); and the Byzantine Empire. Following a period of Islamization, the Ottoman Turks captured Constantinople and created an expansive empire that lasted until World War I. Under Mustafa Kemal Atatürk, Turkey was established in 1923 as a secular republic that represented an Islamic majority but embraced Western civil law and dress.[29] Although mostly located in the Middle East, Turkey maintains strong ties to Europe and the West through NATO membership, an US military base on Turkish soil, and ongoing efforts to join the EU. Today, Turkey boasts a top twenty economy in the world. While economic and political upheaval has challenged stability in the past forty years, Turkey enjoys a strong democratic tradition. The government today faces multiple ongoing challenges: responding to Kurdish demands for autonomy, balancing secularism with Islam, establishing widespread and consistent economic-growth strategies, and addressing the pressing needs of a population reeling from natural disasters like the earthquake that struck eastern Turkey in October 2011.

Culture

Turkish culture reflects growing connections to modernity and European values along with established ties to traditional values and Islam. The family remains at the center of Turkish life, with Islam reinforcing that value. Interdependence and support for family members are emphasized rather than self-reliance and individualism. Although the secular state promotes egalitarianism, widespread protection of legal rights, literacy, and education, Turkey remains a patriarchal society. Loyalty to one's family, school, or regional group is valued over individual achievement and assertiveness. Individual performance is not emphasized, although educational attainment is. Relationships between superiors and subordinates remain somewhat formal and hierarchical;

leaders expect obedience from employees, and employees are reluctant to disagree with leaders.

Establishing Culture3 Dialogue

Spend time developing strong personal relationships before beginning business discussions. Because top management in many businesses is a family affair, getting to know a potential colleague's background, family, and personal interests will go a long way in developing a working relationship of trust. Finding ways to utilize in-group relationships will also provide opportunities for growth and expansion. Be decisive, charismatic, and team oriented while regularly consulting with a close nucleus of associates. Maintain social distance from subordinates, but demonstrate holistic concern for their needs and their families' needs. Provide action-oriented, hands-on, and collective-achievement-oriented direction.

United Arab Emirates

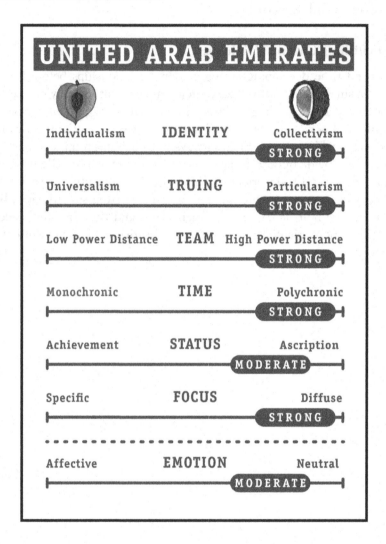

Highlights

Like other countries in the Middle East, the United Arab Emirates (UAE) holds Coconut values. This federation of monarchies is strongly polychronic. Family and in-group relationships as well as personal needs make time commitments flexible. Rather than pursuing tasks along a linear path, multitasking and managing several demands at once are typical. Loyalty to family and in-group members is expected; citizens of the UAE (known as Emiratis) may set aside social rules and regulations to benefit family. The UAE is strongly collectivist, and high power distance is seen as a normal quality of society. Significant overlap occurs between private and public life. Competitiveness among males is another core component of Emirati culture.

History

Located along the southern shore of the Persian Gulf, the UAE is made up of seven emirates, each named after its principal city. The UK established rule over the emirates in the nineteenth century. Despite the discovery of oil in the UAE in 1958, the UK eventually withdrew, and the UAE became a cohesive nation in 1971. Because of the labor demands stemming from its position as a major oil producer, the UAE's foreign-worker population is larger than its native population. The UAE has implemented modest democratic reform; half of the forty-seat Federal National Council is subject to contested elections. In pursuit of becoming a world economic leader, the UAE has changed its weekends to match those of the West, become one of the biggest shareholders on the London Stock Exchange, and built the world's tallest building.

Culture

Despite a strong commitment to Westernization, the UAE maintains traditional values rooted in tribal and family heritage. Education is highly valued; degrees provide status and draw respect from others. Emiratis expect and accept high-power-distance leadership. It is normal for leaders to separate themselves from their subordinates, yet those same leaders are expected to exercise paternal leadership in the hierarchically stratified Emirati society. Commitments to groups and relationships endure whether at work or outside of work, a practice that keeps society functioning and provides structure, roles, and responsibilities for everyone.

Establishing Culture3 Dialogue

Spend time developing strong relationships of trust before conducting business. Be prepared to share information about your background, family, and interests and to learn similar facts about your counterparts. Maintain separation from subordinates and give complete, specific directives. Efforts to promote change through democratic means will be less successful than reinforcing the power distance between supervisors/managers and subordinates.

United Kingdom

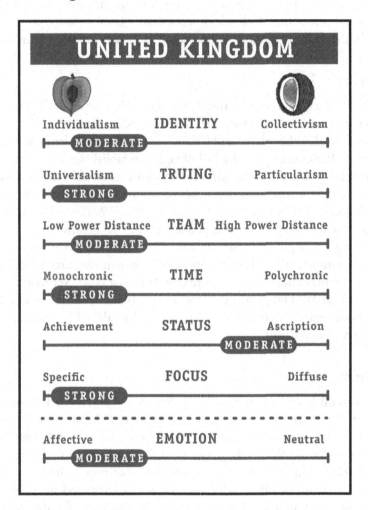

Highlights

UK culture is primarily Peach. Citizens see time as a precious commodity. It is budgeted, managed with deadlines, and evaluated for greater efficiency. Honoring time commitments demonstrates loyalty to the job and respect for others. Universal rules govern behavior and structure personal interactions. In negotiation and persuasion, reason and rationality are often invoked. Although high power distance was historically the norm, modern preferences for low power distance have made relationships less formal. There are distinct divisions between work and private life. Individual performance is increasingly important. Public displays of emotion are becoming more acceptable, within limits.

History

The UK came into being through acts of union between England and other nations in the British Isles: Wales (1535), Scotland (1707), and Ireland (1801, although most of Ireland regained independence in 1922[30]). In 1689, Parliament passed a bill of rights, establishing a constitutional monarchy and making the king and queen accountable to Parliament. The UK was the first country to establish colonies around the world and to industrialize. Under Queen Victoria's rule (1837–1901), the UK solidified a traditional class system and expanded its colonial holdings.

Though a popular saying claimed that "the sun never sets on the British Empire," the UK ended its colonial expansion after World War I. The country later played a key role in defeating Nazi Germany during World War II. The postwar period was characterized by the development of a welfare state based upon collectivist values like tolerance and equality of opportunity.

Culture

The traditional British class system (developed and refined throughout Queen Victoria's reign) once dictated appropriate behavior and obligations. Violation of social rules led to dishonor and possible ostracism. Following World War II, however, the UK changed rapidly as the result of increased immigration from across the Commonwealth, the rise to power of progressively minded baby boomers, increased regional- and ethnic-identity politics that gave rise to institutions like the Scottish Parliament, and a major shift in cultural values. Today, the UK is experiencing clashes between an enduring (but declining) traditional class system and an emerging liberal culture. Traditional values like authoritarian leadership, high power distance, status gained from birth and education, and emotional reserve or maintaining "a stiff upper lip" prevail. However, many of the younger generation reject high power distance, challenge class-based behavioral norms, and support status based on merit.

Establishing Culture3 Dialogue

Provide leadership that emphasizes individual performance. Provide regular encouragement to inspire motivation and improve execution. Presenting visionary leadership while maintaining moderate power distance will garner respect from employees. Act in ways that demonstrate your personal abilities and commitment to excellence. Promptness, structure, and organization will go far in sending a message of strong leadership.

United States of America

U. S. A.

Individualism	**IDENTITY**	Collectivism
STRONG		
Universalism	**TRUING**	Particularism
STRONG		
Low Power Distance	**TEAM**	High Power Distance
STRONG		
Monochronic	**TIME**	Polychronic
STRONG		
Achievement	**STATUS**	Ascription
STRONG		
Specific	**FOCUS**	Diffuse
STRONG		
Affective	**EMOTION**	Neutral
MODERATE		

Highlights

US culture is solidly Peach. Based on the uniquely US ideal that anyone can get ahead if he or she works hard enough (known as the American dream), status is determined primarily by individual achievement. Time plays a strong role in determining action; behavior is structured by deadlines. Grounded by their commitment to universal rights, they generally believe that all people should be treated equally regardless of economic situation, position in society, gender, etc. This value keeps power distance low.

History

To understand core US values, one has to start with the historical context in which the country was formed. Through colonial experiences, the American Revolution, and finally achieving independence (declared in 1776 but not internationally recognized until 1783)[31], a uniquely US sense of self and mission developed. The acts of breaking free from oppression, working together to settle an untamed landscape, forming a government "of the people"[32] that restricted autocratic use of power, and taking individual responsibility for one's own welfare all contributed to the formation of a society dedicated to progress and the expansion of rights. The US Civil War, the Industrial Revolution, universal suffrage, and the Civil Rights Movement all resulted from and built upon these core values. Economic progress and the sense of a universal mission led the US to emerge from World War II as a military and economic superpower. While the US military and economy have declined relative to those of other countries, the US continues to play a key role in the health of the world economy, technological innovation, global security, and the spread of democratic and consumer values and popular culture.

Culture

With the third-largest population on Earth—largely made up of immigrants and descendants of immigrants from all over the world—the US holds distinct Peach values, including self-determination, patriotism, and equality. Social mobility is prized and seen as a contributing factor to "the good society." Individuals are expected to be innovative, speak up for themselves, and favor individualism over conformity. While the American Dream is seen by some to be no longer achievable, many people still see the US as a "light on a hill" and the guardian of democracy and freedom. Leaders are expected to excel in personal achievement, provide leadership for change, inspire others with optimism, act decisively and quickly, and stay true to their core beliefs.

Establishing Culture3 Dialogue

Appeals to individualism, self-determination, and merit will have the most success in motivating change. US employees view working as a team as a blending of individual efforts rather than as a single unit putting forth a group effort. Be optimistic, provide clear vision, encourage participation in decision-making processes, and show respect for each person regardless of position, ethnicity, background, etc. Honor time commitments, allow for risk taking, and develop a results-oriented work culture. To do so, focus on individual action and responsibility and build and maintain low power distance, especially when promoting organizational change.

Vietnam

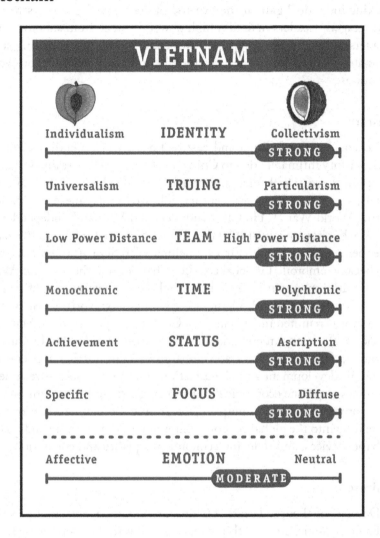

Highlights

Vietnam has a Coconut culture. It is strongly polychronic. Vietnamese people often compromise punctuality and meeting deadlines to accommodate important duties to family, friends, and others in their social networks. Status comes from age, position, and family background. When learning of new resources, information, and opportunities, Vietnamese people act in ways that promote the welfare of their own social groups. Seeking individual gain at the expense of one's social group is strongly discouraged. Leaders maintain high power distance from subordinates. Leaders' authority permeates both work and private life, requiring subordinates to demonstrate respect for that authority even in non-work situations.

History

Located south of China and east of Laos and Cambodia, Vietnam had a history intimately tied to China until it defeated invading Chinese troops in the year 939. Vietnam came under French colonial rule in the latter part of the nineteenth century, followed by Japanese occupation during World War II. Ho Chi Minh declared Vietnam's independence in 1945, but it wasn't until 1954 that France gave up its claim to Vietnam after being defeated in the First Indochina War. Shortly afterwards, the US became embroiled in local conflicts that became the Vietnam War, finally withdrawing in 1972. Following three more years of fighting between West-backed South Vietnam and Communist North Vietnam, the country was reunited in 1976 under a Communist government. Starting in the 1980s, Vietnam embarked on a program of reform and industrialization. The US lifted a trade embargo in 1994, further accelerating economic development and liberalization. The Vietnamese government continues to pursue economic development by attracting foreign investment, promoting private enterprise, integrating the Vietnamese economy more fully into the global economy, improving infrastructure and access to basic services, and reducing economic inequality and corruption.

Culture

Despite one thousand years of Chinese domination, one hundred years of French colonialism, and thirty years of civil war, the Vietnamese feel a deep sense of national pride. Progenitors are venerated through ancestor worship. Though patriotism is linked to historical memory, Vietnamese people are future oriented. Society is carefully ordered and stratified. All people have specific roles and duties in any given social situation that require them to show or receive respect based on age, social status, and group memberships. Starting with the family, the group is an important unit in Vietnamese society. As in other Asian cultures, maintaining group cohesiveness is closely connected with saving face, including not embarrassing or humiliating someone in public.

Establishing Culture3 Dialogue

Show sincere respect for age and authority. Refrain from interacting casually or informally with subordinates, colleagues, and superiors. Acting in ways that save face is essential. For instance, complimenting a business and its leaders for their hospitality and successes is a way to save face. On the other hand, publicly correcting individual behavior or pointing out flaws in a company will cause others to lose face.

BIBLIOGRAPHY

Bennett, Milton J., ed. *Basic Concepts of Intercultural Communication*. Yarmouth, ME: Intercultural Press, 1998.

Bohm, David. *On Dialogue*. New York: Routledge, 1996.

Campbell, Joseph. *The Hero with a Thousand Faces*. Princeton: Princeton University Press, 2004.

Chen, Guo-Ming, and William J. Starosta, eds. *Communication and Global Society*. New York: Peter Lang, 2000.

Chen, Guo-Ming, and William J. Starosta. *Foundations of Intercultural Communication*. Lanham, MD: University Press of America, 2005.

Eze, Michael Onyebuchi (2008). "What is African Comunitarianism? Against consensus as a regulative Ideal", *South African Journal of Philosophy*, Vol. 27:4, pp. 386–399

Freire, Paulo. 1972. *Pedagogy of the oppressed*. [New York]: Herder and Herder.

Hall, Edward T. *The Silent Language*. Garden City, NY: Doubleday, 1959.

Hammond, S. C., K. Cissna, and R. Anderson. "The Problematics of Dialogue as Empowerment." *Communication Yearbook* (27) (2003): .

Hammond, S. C., and L. Glenn. "Social Network Theory and the Chinese Concept of Guanxi." *Emergence* (6, 2) (2004): .

Hammond, Scott C., and Rene Houston. "The Prison with Symbolic Walls: Complexity and Structuration in Havel's *Power of the Powerless*." *Tamara: Journal of Critical Postmodern Organization Science* 1, no. 4 (2001): 47–59. https://tamarajournal.com/index.php/tamara/article/view/47/42.

Hammond, S. C., and Matthew L. Sanders. "Dialogue as Social Self-Organization: An Introduction." *Emergence* 4, no. 4 (2003): .

Hofstede, G., G. Hofstede, and M. Minkov. *Cultures and Organizations: The Software of the Mind*. New York: McGraw-Hill, 2010.

Hofstede, Gert Jan, Paul B. Pederson, and Geert Hofstede. *Exploring Culture*. Boston: Intercultural Press, 2002.

Ho, David Yao-Fai. "Face, Social Expectations, and Conflict Avoidance." In *Readings in Cross-Cultural Psychology; Proceedings of the Inaugural Meeting of the International Association for Cross-Cultural Psychology*

Held in Hong Kong, August 1972, edited by John Dawson and Walter Lonner, 240–51. Hong Kong University Press, 1974.

Ho, David Yau-Fai. "On the Concept of Face." *American Journal of Sociology* 81, no. 4 (1976): 867–84.

Kuhn, Thomas S. *The Structure of Scientific Revolutions*. Chicago: University of Chicago Press, 1970.

Lewis, Richard D. *The cultural imperative*. Boston: Intercultural Press, 2003.

Lewis, Richard D. *Humor across Frontiers*. Hampshire: Transcreen Publications, 2005.

Lewis, Richard D. *When Cultures Collide*. Boston: Intercultural Press, 2006.

Lord, Bette Bao. *Legacies: A Chinese Mosaic*. New York: Random House, 1991.

Martin, Judith N., and Thomas K. Nakayama. *Intercultural Communication in Contexts*. 4th ed. New York: McGraw-Hill, 2007.

Stahl, Günter K., Martha L. Maznevski, Andreas Voigt, and Karsten Jonsen. "Unraveling the Effects of Cultural Diversity in Teams: A Meta-Analysis of Research on Multicultural Work Groups." *Journal of International Business Studies* 41, no. 4 (2010): 690–709.

Storti, Craig. *Cross-Cultural Dialogues*. Boston: Intercultural Press, 1994.

Ting-Toomey, S. "The Matrix of Face: An Updated Face-Negotiation Theory." In *Theorizing about Intercultural Communication*, edited by W. B. Gudykunst, 71–92. Thousand Oaks, CA: Sage, 2005.

Trompenaars, Fons, and Charles Hampden-Turner. *Riding the Waves of Culture: Understanding Diversity in Global Business*. 2nd ed. New York: McGraw-Hill, 1998.

Yutang, Lin (1935). *My Country and My People* (Hardcover). New York: Reynal & Hitchcock. pp. 199–200

ENDNOTES

1   Bette Bao Lord, *Legacies: A Chinese Mosaic* (New York: Ballantine Books, 1991), 3.

2   Günter K. Stahl et al., "Unraveling the Effects of Cultural Diversity in Teams: A Meta-Analysis of Research on Multicultural Work Groups." *Journal of International Business Studies* 41, no. 4 (2010): 690–709.

3   Both students' accounts have been edited for grammar, punctuation, and clarity.

4   Campbell, Joseph. 2004. *The hero with a thousand faces*. Princeton, N.J.: Princeton University Press.

5   *Kuhn, Thomas S. The Structure of Scientific Revolutions. Chicago: University of Chicago Press, 1970.*

6   Max Fisher, "The Five Craziest Moments from Gary Locke's Tenure as U.S. Ambassador to China," *Washington Post*, November 20, 2013, https://www.washingtonpost.com/news/worldviews/wp/2013/11/20/the-five-craziest-moments-from-gary-lockes-tenure-as-u-s-ambassador-to-china/?utm_term=.9a4909aae015.

7   Hall, Edward T. 1959. *The silent language*. Garden City, N.Y.: Doubleday.

8   Stephen R. Covey, *The 7 Habits of Highly Effective People: Lessons in Personal Change*. New York: Free Press, 1989.

9   This account has been edited for grammar, punctuation, and clarity.

10 This account has been edited for grammar, punctuation, and clarity.

11 Brown, Bert, *Negotiations, social-psychological perspectives*, edited by Daniel Druckman, Sage Publications, Beverly Hills, 1977, Page 275.

12 Yutang, Lin (1935). *My Country and My People* (Hardcover). New York: Reynal & Hitchcock. pp. 199–200

13 UbuntuPlanet.org   https://connect.ubuntuplanet.org/status/9807/, Accessed 26 May 2018.

14 *New World Encyclopedia*, "Ubuntu (philosophy)," http://www.newworldencyclopedia.org/entry/Ubuntu (philosophy), Accessed 27 May 2018.

15 Eze, Michael Onyebuchi. 2010 *Intellectual History in Contemporary South Africa*. New York: Palgrave Macmillan.

16 Fombad, Charles M. 2017. *Constitutional Adjudication in Africa*. Oxford: Oxford University Press

17 Freire, Paulo. 1972. *Pedagogy of the oppressed*. [New York]: Herder and Herder.

18 "The Declaration of Independence, 1776," Milestones: 1776–1783, United States Department of State, accessed December 29, 2017, https://history.state.gov/milestones/1776-1783/declaration (site no longer maintained).

19 Abraham Lincoln, "The Gettysburg Address," November 19, 1863, Avalon Project, Yale University, transcript, http://avalon.law.yale.edu/19th_century/gettyb.asp.

Printed in the United States
By Bookmasters